LIVE
BEYOND

Published by Forefront Books.

Cover Design by Bruce Gore, Gore Studio Inc.
Interior Design by Bill Kersey, KerseyGraphics

ISBN: 978-1-948677-42-4
ISBN: 978-1-948677-43-1 (eBook)

Author's note: the names of certain people have been changed.

LIVE BEYOND

A RADICAL CALL TO SURRENDER AND SERVE

DAVID VANDERPOOL MD

Forefront
BOOKS

DEDICATION

*For my beautiful wife, Laurie, who has been
with me every step of the way.*

ACKNOWLEDGMENTS

To Laurie: This book would not have been possible without the unending support of my beautiful wife, Laurie. Throughout our wonderful thirty-nine years together, we have grown madly in love with each other and the Lord God whom we serve. It is truly an honor to serve in the Kingdom beside you.

To David, John Mark, and Jacklyn: Thanks to the three best kids the world has ever seen. When you were young, you lugged medical bags to the remote corners of the world to help provide care to the needy. Now you are serving God mightily in your own ways!

To Devin, Lauren, and Connor: Thanks for your loving commitment to my children, great suggestions for stories for this book, and wonderful wordcraft.

To Gene Stallings, my father-in-law: Thanks for encouraging me to become a surgeon since I was too slow for football, and because I knew there had to be an easier way to make a living than ranching.

To Mrs. Ruth Ann: Thanks for raising such a wonderful girl.

To Johnny: Thanks for teaching us about unconditional love.

To Mom and Dad: Thanks for lovingly bringing me up in the Grace of our Lord Jesus and for setting me on my path.

To Jackie and John: Thanks for your constant support, hospitality, and the use of your lake house, a place of quiet rest, to finish writing this book.

To Anna Lee, Tim, Martha Kate, and Keith: Thanks for putting up with our re-entry culture shock.

To my teachers at St. Mark's School of Texas:

Mr. J.J. Connolly, my favorite English teacher at St. Mark's, thanks for inspiring me to write.

Mr. Bennet, whose senior year classics class inspired my love of words.

Ms. Colby, whose years of teaching me high school French have paid off richly in Haiti. *Merci beaucoup.*

To Drs. Pelley and Dalley: Thanks for believing in me.

To Steve Green, literary agent extraodinaire: Thanks for your encouragement to continue the process.

To Jonathan Merkh: Thanks for taking a chance publishing a first-time author. May there be many more!

To Billie Brownell: Thanks for your patient and gentle editing of my first attempt at writing a book.

To John: Thanks for giving your life to serve your people; your death was not in vain.

To Solomon, Bryan, Vankat, and Bala: Thanks for your hard work and vision.

To our eighty strong LiveBeyond Haitian staff members: Thanks; you believed God would transform your community.

To all the LiveBeyond volunteers: Thanks for helping us make it a reality.

And most importantly, thanks to Jesus Christ our Lord and Savior without whom none of this is possible.

CONTENTS

CHAPTER 1

HEARING THE CALL – THE EARTHQUAKE

To live beyond means to follow God's calling wherever He leads.

THE SCENE RESEMBLED HELL ON EARTH.

Hundreds of patients lay on the hard floor, screaming for help and writhing in pain from shattered limbs and crushed bodies. Their collective stories of loss filled the hospital like the rubble filled the streets. Many had lost everyone. Everyone had lost someone: husbands, wives, mothers, fathers, brothers, sisters, daughters, and sons. They all had names, hopes, and aspirations until that Tuesday, January 12, 2010, when the world around them crumbled in a moment.

I arrived in Haiti two days after the earthquake with my two sons, David and John Mark. As I surveyed the hundreds of people waiting to be treated, I knew they vastly outnumbered our meager resources. My expertise as a surgeon would be vital, but I wondered, *What have I gotten us into?*

Two days earlier, while sitting in my office in the leafy Nashville suburb of Brentwood, Tennessee, making the decision to go had been complicated. The initial reports were staggering: a 7.0 earthquake had leveled much of Port-au-Prince, leaving 330,000 people dead, even more wounded, a city torn apart, a country decimated. I scrolled through report after report online, the images on my computer screen confirming the horror. I knew I should go.

But . . . I can't just leave, can I? Is it time to go overseas again? Questions of doubt wracked my brain as I considered all the implications of dropping everything and running to provide disaster relief in Haiti. My disaster relief organization, LiveBeyond, was putting the finishing touches on a medical clinic in Honduras.

What about my medical practice? What about my patients who have been scheduled for months? Haven't I already been away from my practice and my family too much lately?

But what about the thousands of patients desperately waiting for help in Haiti? Don't I owe them my skills in this time of need?

This silent debate continued in my mind as I drove home through our picturesque neighborhood, past my children's private school nestled in the hardwoods at the foot of the stunning Middle Tennessee hills, where my wife, Laurie, and I enjoyed our sons' football games and our daughter Jacklyn's track meets. As usual, I had to fight my selfishness to consider the needs of others above my own. In all honesty, I didn't want to leave my comforts and face the hazards and threats that were sure to come from working in a dangerous environment. I kept asking myself, *Do I really need to leave such comfort for the dangerous undertaking I am considering? Do I really want to subject my family to such peril?*

My musing was broken as Texan, our German shepherd, welcomed me home by jumping into my truck and licking me unceremoniously on the face. As I crossed the bridge that led to our front door, Texan playfully tried to push me into the pond below. The aroma of sizzling steaks wafted from the outdoor grill, and I looked forward to relaxing and spending time with my family: my beautiful wife of twenty-nine years, Laurie, and two of our three children, John Mark and Jacklyn. At that moment, everything in me said that I was crazy to leave such an idyllic home. Surely this was a time when others could step up and take care of the problem at hand.

But I couldn't shake the images I had seen and the questions that lingered in my mind. *What about the people dying in agony under the rubble? What of the mothers and fathers leaving behind children who would face many long, hungry nights ahead?*

Over ribeye steaks, stuffed baked potatoes, and green beans, I shared my dilemma. As I suspected, my whole family was not only clamoring to do their part, but they all wanted to be on the first flight out from Nashville. Midway through dinner, my eldest son, David, who was finishing his senior year at Abilene Christian University, called my cellphone.

"Dad, you heard what happened?"

"Yep. It's bad, son."

"I know. You going?"

"Yeah, I think I am."

"I am too. I'll meet you in Miami."

To the chagrin of their sixteen-year-old sister, only my two boys (due to their size and age) were nominated to accompany me. That night we booked airline tickets and began packing surgical equipment and clothes for an undetermined duration in a foreign land. But before I went to bed that night, I confessed to Laurie that I didn't really want to go. In the twelve months prior, I'd been to Mozambique twice and Honduras three times. My surgical practice would suffer, my back hurt, and I was sort of hoping for a break. She kissed my cheek before we prayed. I admitted my reluctance to the Lord and confessed my selfishness. With a tenacity I'd rarely experienced before, I felt His powerful grip. I knew that going was His will for me, and I suddenly wanted to go more than I wanted to stay. In fact, I wanted to go more than anything else in the world.

———

The next day, I made some calls. The first was to Dr. Clint Doiron, a friend of a friend, who had built a hospital and orphanage on the border of Haiti and the Dominican Republic. He offered us the use of his buildings during our stay. His hospital and base seemed to have been custom-made for the upcoming task at hand. Then I called my excellent office staff, who had become accustomed to rescheduling my patients for weeks on end after I started Mobile Medical Disaster Relief in 2005. Many times a disaster had occurred in some remote part of the world, and we had packed up and left on a moment's notice—similar to what I was now doing—leaving my staff to scramble to revamp my busy days. Amazingly, both my staff and patients were not only understanding but, also supportive of my efforts, even when it led to their inconvenience.

John Mark and I finished packing and rushed to the airport, where the American Airlines agent eyed us warily as we struggled to drag eleven bags stuffed with surgical equipment to the counter. Her eyes popped when she saw the electronic scale register well over a hundred pounds per bag. But her protests subsided when I explained our mission. With her supervisor's approval, our overweight bags were sent on their way to Santo Domingo, Dominican Republic. Because the Port-au-Prince airport was damaged in the earthquake, we would have to fly into the Dominican Republic and drive to the Haitian border to respond to the disaster. After a quick flight from Nashville, John Mark and I met David at the Miami airport.

The Caribbean loomed large as we watched Florida disappear beneath our wings. The excitement of packing and the surge of the upcoming adventure began to wane as the impact of our decision began to sink in. Uncertainty in our Nashville suburb usually centered on the rise and fall of the stock market or the final score of a football game. Now we were looking into the unknown, and it had teeth.

It was after dark when we touched down in Santo Domingo and loaded a rental car with our equipment. We had ordered a larger vehicle, but the influx of relief workers caused errors at the rental company, so we ended up crowding into a tiny car. It's a wonder that the vehicle didn't break down immediately under the weight. The car struggled under the heavy load, tilted back so that the headlights shone heavenward at a 45-degree angle, making the hairpin turns on the Dominican roads exceptionally hard to navigate.

As we bobbed and weaved our way through the countryside, we noticed many locals sitting along the road, laughing as we went by. We soon realized the source of their mirth was the massive speed bumps in their villages, which we would hit blindly. I began to wonder how much longer the suspension on our vehicle would last.

We finally reached the hospital as the eastern sky registered the dawn of a new day. We entered the front door and were greeted by two exhausted Dominican nurses and Greg and Chris, Dr. Doiron's right-hand men at the hospital, who led us to the large room that served as the emergency ward. That's when I saw the sight that can only be described as hell on earth. As overwhelmed as we all felt, the sights and sounds around us validated our decision to come.

———

I thought that I was just coming to work in Haiti for a few weeks to provide disaster relief. In fact, I was a little bit proud of myself for following the Lord's lead to leave my comfortable life, my wife, and my daughter to work with the suffering. I was willing to submit to these conditions for a week or two at a time. Little did I know that weeks would turn into months, and three years later, Haiti would become my permanent home. Little did I know that when the Lord gripped me to go in 2010, it was a permanent grip.

When people ask how my wife and I decided to give up my medical practice, sell our home and belongings, and move to Haiti, I find it difficult to answer. It was a gut-wrenching process. I'd like to say that it was easy. I knew the picture Jesus painted of His committed followers, but the truth was that I enjoyed my status and the comforts of life that came with being a surgeon. I enjoyed quiet evenings with my family and being surrounded by godly neighbors and friends. I enjoyed my work, church, restaurants, and college football. I had to fight my own desires in order to let Jesus's call conquer my life. I wanted to submit to His complete will, but at the same time, I wanted to live by my own design. The truth was that I enjoyed keeping one foot in the world while my other foot followed Him to disaster areas of Africa, Central America, or inner-city America. I liked to talk about the way we all should *live beyond* ourselves, our culture, our borders, and even our own lives, but living beyond myself proved to be a struggle. Practicing what I preached was not at all easy.

I knew that Jesus was my perfect example. In order to come to earth in the days of His flesh, He gave up His riches, His power, and His glory and left His family. He lived as a poor man and died a horrible death. Yet for me, it wasn't an easy decision to leave what I had in order to become more like Him. Answering His call to serve in Thomazeau, Haiti, and choosing to live beyond the status quo to join Jesus in relieving the pain of the oppressed has proven to be rewarding and fulfilling yet extremely humbling.

I happen to believe that His radical call is for every Christian.

This call is His invitation to leave our old lifestyle behind in order to become like Him. He didn't exclude anyone when He commanded His followers to "Go."

Throughout Scripture, we read the commands to sell our possessions, to leave our families, to go into the world, to serve the poor, to protect the oppressed, and to preach the Gospel. But for my entire life, I read these Scriptures thinking they applied to someone else. The day I realized this was a call to me shook me to my core. Answering this radical call meant choosing to live like Jesus, the perfect model for everyone who chooses to live beyond.

But the decision to serve full-time in Haiti didn't occur overnight. The Lord had begun stirring my heart and preparing me for this task decades earlier. In fact, it all started in my childhood.

CHAPTER 2

LAYING THE
FOUNDATION

*To live beyond means to look back at where
you started—and then aim beyond that.*

My parents had a huge impact on my life's calling to become a medical missionary. It was their influence on me at a young age that made me want to live by example just as they did. My parents did everything they could to "bring [me] up in the discipline and instruction of the Lord" (Ephesians 6:4).

My mother came from a socially prominent family in Dallas. Her father was an insurance executive. During the Great Depression, he had a stroke. The Depression and World War II hit their family hard because of his illness. So my mother always understood the value of hard work and never took anything for granted. She received her teaching degree from Southern Methodist University shortly before meeting my father.

My father's family were not people of means. They moved around frequently due to my grandfather's job as a druggist. My father is highly intelligent—he graduated high school at 15, college at 19, and medical school at 23. He trained at Parkland Hospital in Dallas, Texas, for his surgical residency before joining the Air Force. He became a well-respected surgeon and served as president of the Texas Medical Association and on the Board of Governors of the American Medical Association. He was politically connected through the success of his medical career.

But even a man so successful as he took on some interesting jobs because of his commitment to service. During his residency, he served as the Dallas County Jail doctor; he even slept in a jail cell. When he started dating my mother, he decided to place membership at Preston Road Church of Christ. He listed his resident address as the jail address, much to the chagrin of the preacher and his own mother. My mother and father married in 1955. When I was young, my father served the church by visiting missionaries with illnesses to help determine if they would need immediate medical attention in the United States or if they could be treated locally. Both of my parents have always had a heart for service. My mother has always excelled at organizing packing parties and other service opportunities with her friends from church.

I was born in 1960 to this stable, loving Christian family. The Lord has surrounded me with His people my entire life. From church youth group to a Christian college, I've had every opportunity to hear and know the truth. I have never wanted for anything, went to the best schools, and had everything I needed and more.

As a boy, I often traveled overseas with my family to places where poverty could not be hidden. I encountered children begging in places like Cairo, Egypt, and Bogotá, Columbia. At first, the constant sight of the beggars' upturned hands and pitiful expressions surprised me. But eventually, I realized that these children had nothing. If they wanted to eat, they had to beg. Many were orphans left to fend for themselves. I had read about them in books and been taught to care for them in Sunday School, but what could a young boy like me do for them?

The aftermath of one particular trip is highlighted in my memory.

It was 1976 and the first day of my junior year of high school.

As I pulled into the parking lot of the boy's college-preparatory school I attended in Dallas, the radio in my new car blared "Fortunate Son" by Creedence Clearwater Revival. Apparently, my friends' car radios were tuned to the same station because the song reverberated throughout the parking lot. As we sat rocking out in our cars, reveling in the music, the irony was totally lost on us that we were the fortunate sons the singer railed at. We were the sons of prominent doctors, lawyers, and industry titans. We were "born, silver spoon in hand," eager to enjoy the best life had to offer: Aspen ski vacations, the sunny Riviera, Ivy League educations.

But I was unsettled. I quickly switched off the radio to silence the music, not because I didn't like it but because its truth was finally starting to register. Two weeks before, I had been in São Paulo, Brazil, on a journey through South America with my family. We had visited the Favela do Moinho, one of the largest slums in the world. This slum was surrounded by a wall built to hide the unpleasant sight of the people inside, but the barrier did little to hide the stench of their suffering.

As we entered the gates a cold rain fell, and I saw, for the first time, in the eyes of people at the nadir of despair, what unrelenting poverty looks like. I was shocked to see tens of thousands of people living on the mud-slicked hillside in nothing more than cardboard boxes. Smoke rose from the dung-fueled cooking fires and settled in the hollows of the expansive slum.

Our first contact with the inhabitants was with the children. Lured from their cardboard hideouts by their insatiable curiosity, they surrounded us, apparently unafraid of these strange Americans invading their inhospitable world. They were dressed in ill-fitting shirts, their grotesquely protruding bellies masking their severe malnutrition. Our Portuguese-speaking friend began to entertain them with magic tricks and candy, and slowly even the adults were drawn to our growing circle.

As if the children weren't shocking enough, the adults who lived here were truly hanging on to life by their ragged nails. Their ribs showed through mud-caked shirts, and the hollows of their cheeks reminded me of pictures of death camp survivors. Their eyes, though, told the full story: generations of torment, hunger, and death; countless children lost to starvation; the relentless destruction of their cardboard homes by the wind and rain; and their ultimate degradation by abject poverty.

Back home in Dallas, I knew I would never forget what I had witnessed. As I left the parking lot for my first class of the day, the memory of those Brazilian eyes went with me, a haunting reminder of the wide gulf fixed between us.

Why was I born into a life of relative luxury and success while so many people in the world live like those in the favela? Why was I given loving parents who surrounded me with everything necessary for success? Why was I not born into a horrific slum and one of them born into a life of ease?

Years later, rock superstar Bono would call this the "accident of latitude." Whatever name you give to the disparity, I discovered on that summer trip that the cry of suffering that is inaudible in our comfortably excessive lifestyles becomes overwhelmingly loud—and, for me, unforgettable—whenever we dare to venture beyond our protective walls.

On these family trips the harsh realities of the real world crashed into the fragile sphere of affluence to which I was accustomed. I realized just how fortunate I was—and it began to trouble me. *Why did the Lord put me in a loving family with more than enough money and many possessions while other people didn't even know where their next meal would come from?*

I didn't have an answer to that question and soon learned that no one else did either. This gap between people who had a lot and people who had nothing bothered me. As I grew older, I realized it wasn't just food, clothes, new cars, and nice houses that other people didn't have; they also lacked the opportunity and means to change their situation.

—

When I was sixteen, I visited the Middle East for the first time. My family was in Nazareth, Israel, worshipping with local believers. After church services one evening, I found myself talking on the front steps of the church with Fadila, a very intelligent Israeli girl about my own age. Getting to know Fadila and hearing about her life and family was incredibly humbling. She was articulate and clever.

As we got acquainted, we began to share a bit about our lives and our futures. "You are lucky, David," she said in perfect English, "and I envy you with your many options. You will be able to choose your future and what you do with your life— where you go to university, your career, where you live."

"Well, sure," I said. "But you've got your whole life ahead of you too."

"It's not the same," she replied. "My family is poor, and I am a female. I'm destined to marry early and bear children."

"But you are so smart! You could be a doctor or attorney or teacher or whatever you want to be!" I might not have admitted it at the time, but I knew that Fadila was probably smarter than I.

"It does not matter what I want to be," she said. "That's my point." She sighed and looked away. "You have options for your life that are not open to me."

I swallowed hard. There was nothing I could say. I recognized injustice. Here was one of the brightest people I had ever met, and yet she was trapped by circumstances beyond her control.

Something about this encounter stirred me. I think the Lord was planting a seed. He was making me uncomfortable. I started to ask myself, *Will I work only for my own success, or will I remember the needs of those who had not been given the advantages I'd been handed and find ways to live beyond myself for them?*

"Living beyond" means to look back at where you started and then aim far beyond that. I acknowledge that I started my life's trajectory with extraordinary advantages: loving parents, a functional family, a good education, the chance to travel, all the material possessions I needed, and a Christian worldview that helped me not only to stay on the "straight and narrow," but that gave me a grateful heart and a willingness to give back. My family had a certain vision for what my life would be as a respected surgeon. But as life went on, I started to feel called beyond even the very high dreams that my family had for me. Life started in Dallas, Texas, but I soon found it went far beyond my hometown.

Some people will start their life journeys in a very different place. Perhaps a broken home destroyed your family and undermined your foundation. Perhaps you didn't get into the college or have the career that you envisioned. Perhaps disease or debt handicapped your beginnings. Still, "living beyond" means looking at whatever God gives you, the good and the bad, and the circumstances of where you are *right now*, and asking how God might use that background and this present moment in His extraordinary plan for your life. Believe me, He put you on this earth at a particular time and in a particular place and with particular gifts for a reason. All you have to do is look for the clues all around you.

A life marred by divorce? Perhaps He's called you to break that generational curse and build a strong marriage. Struggling with disease or disability? Maybe God is calling you to be an example for others of how to face this adversity with the confidence that only God can give. Don't have the career you had hoped for? Perhaps God is preparing you for future endeavors you haven't dreamed of yet. Overwhelmed with student loan debt? Maybe God is calling you to manage money responsibly so that you can later use your money to provide for others.

What talents, interests, experiences, relationships, and dreams have shaped you? How might God be shaping those things into a "live beyond" kind of life?

————

However unsettled I was by my glimpses of poverty, realistically I had little to offer the poor at this point in my life. I had no money other than that which was given to me by my parents or that I earned in summer jobs, no particular talent or skill to address the needs I saw, and no clear vision of how I could possibly help. Jesus's call on my life at this point was simply to prepare me for what was ahead. He had planted the seed. It was my job to let it grow.

CHAPTER 3

CHOICES AND CHANGES

*To live beyond means to accept that preparation
is part and parcel of the Master's plan.*

GOING INTO MEDICINE WAS ALMOST AUTOMATIC FOR ME. I DON'T remember spending much time thinking about what I might want to be when I grew up. I just knew I wanted to be a doctor. But not just any doctor—I wanted to be a surgeon just like my dad. I spent as many weekends as possible at the hospital, soaking up everything I could learn at the nurses' station while my dad was on rounds. He was very encouraging about this and even let me tag along to some of his minor procedures. I always enjoyed the sciences, so my exposure to the hospital from a young age made becoming a surgeon a reflexive decision. Every step I took with my education in middle school and high school was to realize my plan to become a surgeon, and my parents were very supportive of my wishes. After graduating from St. Mark's, I went to Abilene Christian University to earn my bachelor's of science in biology. Then I attended Texas Tech University for a Doctorate in Medicine and did my residency at Baylor University Medical Center in Dallas, specializing in surgery.

I realize that not everyone knows exactly what they want to do from such a young age, but God was using even this time to give me all the tools I would need to fulfill His destiny for me. In college and medical school and residency, I never doubted that I would finish and reach my ultimate dream. I was doing what God intended for my life.

I learned so much from God through each step of my surgical residency and early career. From about age sixteen through medical school and residency, God taught me about His sovereignty. "Whatever the Lord pleases, He does, in Heaven and on earth, in the seas and all deeps." (Psalm 135:6) His ways are mysterious, known only to Him, and there is no questioning this. What was often a little harder to accept as I faced mortality each day was that what He does is right. This is the undercurrent of Christian faith. No matter what you're going through, He is in control and He will bring about things for the good of those who love Him (Romans 8:28). He taught me this, as He often does, through hardship. Studying to be a doctor wasn't easy. But just like a muscle grows by tearing down, my faith in His sovereignty grew most in times of difficulties. It was when I tried to avoid hardship that I learned the least.

I was reminded of God's all-powerful nature one day during residency when I walked into the emergency room and saw a man with an ornamental Bowie knife protruding from his chest. It was a massive knife, normally used in displays as a wall mount. The man was also showing definite signs of drug usage, screaming that he was going to kill us and thrashing about, so he had already been restrained prior to his entry into the emergency room. When you walk into Trauma 1 and see something like that, you know it's going to be a bad day at the office.

Before we removed the blade from the man's chest, we needed to see the damage it had done upon entry. We had to know if the knife had severed any arteries or damaged any vital organs that we would need to be prepared for during our surgery. So we utilized the built in X-ray machine to further assess his wounds. This was in the days long before X-ray machines could be rolled about with ease.

For this type of X-ray, the radiology technician was located in a room down the hallway from the X-ray machine. We positioned the man for his X-rays as he continued to shout obscenities and struggle against his restraints. Then we left the room to avoid unnecessary radiation exposure. Almost immediately the X-ray tech came running down the hallway screaming that the man had a gun—she had seen it on the X-ray. Sure enough, we looked back into the room to see him reaching through his restraints for his pocket.

Somehow it fell to me to retrieve the gun. Looking back, I might have even volunteered, not wanting to risk the lives of the nurses. It was a .25 caliber automatic pistol. Thankfully, I was able to safely retrieve the gun with no problems. I knew that God was protecting me through this event; I felt His hand very clearly. And He was protecting the patient, too, because we were able to safely remove the knife from his chest in surgery and patch him up with no further incident.

Another lesson on God's sovereignty was wheeled in on a bloody stretcher one afternoon. A Salvadoran man who worked in a cardboard processing plant had been inside of an industrial shredder clearing a jam when a fellow employee accidentally turned the machine on. This poor guy was mangled beyond belief. None of us really believed he would survive even as we worked to save him. The lower half of his body was pulverized. But in a succession of thirty to forty surgeries over several months we were able to save his life at the cost of his legs. We had to replace his entire blood supply two or three times. But despite overwhelming odds and the risk of infection, the man lived.

Sometime after his initial injury, the residents and doctors who worked on the man were allowed to tour the plant in which the Salvadoran man had worked. It wasn't over a quarter of a mile from the hospital, but we had never known what was in the building. When we saw the shredder that the man had been inside, we were all amazed that he had made it out of the mouth of the machine, much less to the hospital. God had used us, skilled surgeons and nurses, to save this man against all odds because He had given him a future. Our years of training culminated in moments like this, where we worked together to save our fellow man. God fulfilled His promise through our purpose.

Sometimes it felt like God was handing us too much—like the time the 6' 8" Native American man was brought in with tire tracks down his back because his wife had run over him with her car. He started wrestling with me in order to get up and run when she came into the hospital room. Another time we operated on a fireman with a ruptured stomach. He had been thrown from the back of the hook and ladder truck, which was tragic enough, but it was complicated by the fact that he had just eaten a large meal at a local taco joint. I was cleaning chips and jalapeños out of his stomach for hours. But these incidences didn't compare with the time during my residency when I was finishing up a long surgery on a gunshot wound and got a call from my buddy in the operating room next door.

"Dave, come quickly! I need help."

I was exhausted after being on my feet for so long, but I could tell he was serious, so I went to see what was happening. He was performing aortic bifemoral bypass surgery, a surgery he had performed many times before, so I knew that if he was requesting help, it must be serious. I walked into a cloud of chaos and rubble. A workman in the building had fallen through the roof of the operating room while doing some building maintenance. Thankfully, the workman had landed safely next to the patient, but a lot of debris from the roof was now inside the open abdomen of the patient. My fellow doctor, covered in dust, looked frazzled, to say the least. "What do we do, Dave?" There was only one thing to do: we picked out all of the debris, flushed the patient's wound with hundreds of gallons of sterile water, and then my buddy finished the surgery. Miraculously, the patient did well with few complications.

Looking back on the difficulties of medical school and residency, I know that it was preparing me to move to Haiti. Every night was a new adventure during my residency, so what could the stress of Haiti be compared to that? When Laurie and I moved to Thomazeau in 2013, we were sleeping on cots on the unfinished foundation of the guesthouse. We had no clean water, no security, and no electricity. We had to walk in the dark through spider-infested grass to get to the latrines, and we were constantly losing inventory thanks to local thieves. However, it was in these days that we felt God blessing us. We felt His love and His purpose for us being made complete through everything that we did. Our years of preparation were all part of the Master's plan.

CHAPTER 4

FINDING A PARTNER, FOLLOWING A CALLING

To live beyond means finding people with whom you can accomplish more together than you could ever accomplish on your own.

I MARRIED MY MIDDLE SCHOOL SWEETHEART, A BEAUTIFUL, GODLY young lady named Laurie Stallings. We met in 1972 at Prestoncrest Church of Christ. My parents helped start the congregation, and when the Stallings family placed membership, it felt like the size of the church congregation doubled. Standing among her sisters, I singled her out across the room. I still remember that she was wearing a flower print dress. *Man, that's a pretty girl*, I thought. Her family was standing near the front row of pews. I made a beeline down there to meet her. I was 12; she was 13—it was awkward like most interactions are for kids that age. But pretty quickly we became good friends, and our relationship progressed from there—it was natural. When we were old enough, we started dating.

Throughout our dating relationship, Laurie's parents insisted she go to school functions with boys from her own school. They felt it wasn't fair to the boys in her school who had trouble finding dates. I still got to go to a few school functions with her, and I understood where her parents were coming from, but that didn't mean I was ever happy about it. I was protective of Laurie. I might have even secretly followed Laurie on a couple of her dates with other boys. I wasn't exactly jealous (okay, maybe a little)—I just knew how committed I was to Laurie, and I was determined to go to any lengths necessary to protect her if anything went wrong.

Laurie grew up in the most wonderful family I've ever known. Her mother is a very kind and lovely Southern woman. And her family certainly knew about fame because her father is Gene Stallings, the legendary collegiate and NFL football coach. He was a great coach—tough but fair, and he always cared deeply about his players. Winning games was fun—but Coach cared more about how his players presented themselves off the field as students and family members and friends.

Coach did a lot of public speaking while he was coaching for the Cowboys, so sometimes I would drive him so that he could get some rest. It gave us a chance to bond as men. On more than one occasion we were driving to some small-town Fellowship of Christian Athletes banquet, dressed in suits, and we'd see a woman on the side of the road with a flat tire. I knew to pull over right then because Coach insisted that we help these ladies. We would show up to the banquet, late, our suits drenched in sweat with everyone waiting on us, and all he would say was, "Sorry I was late." He didn't want credit for any of his good deeds.

The Stallings family was a father-centric household, a healthy reflection of how our family in Heaven will look. During the off-season, Coach would come home from work on Friday nights and tell everyone, "We're leaving for the ranch in 30 minutes." That meant that the oldest two daughters, Anna Lee and Laurie, usually had to cancel their dates at the last minute and I was often on the receiving end of that cancellation. Then everyone would pile into the car and leave for Paris, Texas, for the weekend. They had about 600 acres outside of this East Texas town. The rule in the family was that for the month of June, any boy who was dating one of the four Stallings daughters was required to work at the ranch for at least a week. I spent many weeks and often the entire month of June sleeping on the couch at the fishing cabin. Coach's goal for the boys who dated his daughters was for us *not* to hang out with the girls. His rigorous schedule made sure of it. We'd work from about 5 a.m. to 9 a.m. welding fences. Mrs. Stallings— Miss Ruth Ann to me—would fix us a champion breakfast. We always left the table feeling like we had food coming out of our ears. After breakfast, we baled hay until we stopped around 3 p.m. for lunch. We then worked the cattle until dinner around 9 p.m., but we couldn't stuff ourselves at dinner as we could at the other meals because we did football training for an hour after dinner before collapsing on the couch for bed. Coach had us run wind-sprints until we were blue in the face. Often, we were cheered on by some of the Dallas Cowboys players who would come out to visit with Coach and watch us work. It was neat getting to spend time on the ranch with the likes of Charlie Waters, Cliff Harris, and Leroy Jordan.

Laurie was the second of five children. The line-up was Anna Lee, Laurie, John Mark, Jackie, and Martha Kate. The four sisters literally and figuratively centered on John Mark, or "Johnny" as he was more widely known. Johnny was born with Down syndrome, and that meant he was the focal point of affection for the family. If Johnny wanted to play a game all of the girls gladly joined in. He was sweet and kind, funny and happy, and everyone doted on him. As a teenager, one of my favorite things to do with Johnny was to take him for a ride in my Jeep to get a Coke or go to Whataburger. He *loved* Whataburger, so we did that a lot.

One of the great things about my relationship with Laurie was that while we both knew what it was like to have material blessings, we shared a strong Christian heritage of faith that included serving those in need. Laurie is the most beautiful, gracious, God-fearing person you will ever meet, traits gleaned from her mother. Laurie is a strong Southern woman with a heart bigger than Texas. If she sees someone in need, she doesn't rest until that need is met.

Shortly after we were married—I was in medical school at the time—an orphanage brought some of the children to our church in Lubbock for Sunday worship. Among the children was a young boy named Cedric. Laurie insisted that he sit with us in church every time he came after that, and although we never tried to get guardianship of him, Laurie somehow managed to get permission to bring him home with us for weekends and special holidays. Through our relationship, we learned that Cedric had seen his father's death and had scars on his back from where his grandmother beat him with an extension cord. His mother was addicted to drugs and was out of the picture. Even after we left Lubbock, we made a point to keep up with Cedric. He lived with us off and on, and now that he's a grown man, we still look forward to hearing from him, checking in with the closest thing he has to a family. Laurie became as close to a mother as he was going to get long before we had kids of our own. And as partners, we were able to do more together than we ever could on our own.

We knew this would be the case even as kids. Laurie's and my skill sets are very different—she is open and warm and friendly while I am generally described as being serious and focused. When it comes to ministry, both of our personalities are useful, and they complement each other. We went on mission trips together in high school from Fort Davis, Texas, to Kentucky. We taught VBS and later devotionals together, and because of our combined talents, they were meaningful to more people than if we had worked alone. Long before we were married, we knew that when we joined our efforts, they didn't just double—they increased exponentially because of how God blessed us together.

———

While dating and marrying Laurie contributed to my decision to start a Christian humanitarian organization and eventually move to Haiti, there's one more experience from those early years of marriage that impacted the way I saw the world.

During my surgical residency, I volunteered with our church congregation to serve food to the homeless population in downtown Dallas. After church, we would load up a panel van with racks of casseroles, peaches, and brownies. Our group would set up beneath an interstate overpass, where hundreds of men and women lined up for food since the local shelters didn't serve on Sundays.

One afternoon as our group was serving food, I encountered someone who stopped me in my tracks. Passing through the line was a young man who could have passed for my brother (if I had one). I literally did a double take. *Why is this guy down here getting free food?* I wondered. He didn't fit my stereotype of a homeless person. He was about my age, wore glasses, looked clean-cut, and was dressed in khakis and a polo shirt.

But when we started talking, I learned that despite how similar we looked, our worlds were very different. Straight out of college, he worked with a large firm, got married, and had a nice home. Then one misfortune after another created a domino effect. After he was laid off from work, his wife divorced him. Then the costs of caring for a family member with a medical problem bankrupted him, forcing him to sell everything to pay off debts. Within a short time, this guy lost his job, his family, and his home. The recession of the early nineties had devastated his market. Every day he worked hard to find another job, any job, but no one was hiring. My naïve assumption that he could just "get a job"—this was America, after all—was disproven as he told me his story. With no other family to turn to, he had ended up on the streets.

Another seed had been planted. I'd previously thought that the homeless were completely different from me. It was a turning point for me to realize how similar we were. I realized that we are the same. We share the same hopes, dreams, and need for love.

This seed planted by the Lord brought more questions. *How can I continue to pursue status, wealth, and comfort while the hundreds lining up in front of me are hungry and living on the streets? Am I really so callous that I can chase the American dream while my fellow brothers and sisters live in squalor?* I was beginning to become uneasy about pursuing the trappings that typically go with the lifestyle of a successful surgeon.

I liked nice things as much as anyone and had definitely grown accustomed to them. But to pursue wealth sounded an awful lot like something I'd read about in the Bible—*idolatry*. I'd known from an early age that "you cannot serve God and money" (Matthew 6:24). But now, I struggled in my own heart with the very real question: Who or what am I going to serve?

CHAPTER 5

THE SUCCESS
OF SACRIFICE

*To live beyond means to sacrifice your own view
of success and instead humbly accept God's
definition of success at each stage of your life.*

I WAS PROGRAMMED FOR SUCCESS. THROUGH HIGH SCHOOL, college, medical school, and residency, it was drilled into me that hard work produces success. So when it came to my 120-hour work week during residency, I thought that it was worth staying up hours on end to the detriment of my health and my family to achieve my goals. I sacrificed a lot during that time in my life, but work was my motivator, my idol. I made less than $22,000 a year during residency, so a lot of nights I would moonlight in an emergency room just to keep us afloat. This workload was on top of my already crushing work schedule.

I remember talking on the phone to a good friend who was a year ahead of me, already in the prestigious partnership that I was planning to join out of residency.

"How is it?" I asked, referring to the partnership. I was expecting to hear about a job with more regular hours, a job in which I might get to see my wife and young sons outside of the wee hours of the morning. I thought I might get more time with my guitar or be able to pursue other interests. His response was not what I wanted to hear.

"It's really busy." This doctor was and still is a machine. He's the best surgeon I've ever been around both technically and intellectually. He can work for days at a time. When I was caught up in the crush of patients and work, he enjoyed it, reveled in the pressure.

"But compared to residency?"

"It's worse."

I went into medical school and residency thinking that a heavy workload in my medical practice would be great, the pathway to success. But that idea was self-aggrandizing. That lifestyle is full of deceit. The problem with this mindset is that it left me with no reliance on God. I approached life with the idea that an incredible workload and busy practice would bring success. I eventually found that this mindset could result in financial gain but my own might and strength would not produce the kind of success I should be striving for.

It's very common for people my age to respond to the question, "How are you?" with "Busy." I may not be accomplishing much, but I like the idea of being busy. I always want to be moving, going, and doing. The problem is that this "busy" lifestyle often leaves no place for God. It means that I am relying too much on my own strength. I did that for five years in residency, working like a madman with no end in sight and no way out. So, after two years of working as a "junior partner" in a super-busy and financially successful surgical practice, I came to the realization that I couldn't continue. It was not possible for me to keep up with the highly demanding pace and have a semblance of the relationship with my family and with God that I desired above all else. My eldest son was six years old, and I had hardly ever seen him awake. My bonding time with him was spent with him curled up on my chest after a long shift at the hospital. He barely knew me. No amount of busyness was worth that. Our two younger children had also been born in these busy years. Laurie was basically raising them as a single mom. So, for the first time I questioned the connection between busyness and my self-worth. I realized that busyness and success are not synonymous. I had the opportunity to be a successful surgeon, but I also wanted to be a successful husband and dad. In my exhaustion, I sensed that I was also not turning out to be so successful in God's eyes. So I made a tough choice. When it came time to become a partner in this practice, I did not accept, despite my ambition and outside pressure. I walked away from all of it. This was an early choice I made to deny my own drive for success and choose a different path to serve God and my family instead of my own ambition and pride.

———

God has blessed Laurie and me by teaching us various lessons during our moves to different cities. Everywhere we lived, we were given a new truth from the Lord. After the residency program in Dallas, while in Jackson, Tennessee, we began to understand the power of the Holy Spirit. The friends we enjoyed and the doctors that I worked with were filled with the Holy Spirit. It was also here that the Lord began to break us of the idea that success is measured by wealth. All of the fancy furniture and fine china didn't matter when compared with the gift of the Holy Spirit. Living below our means began to make far more sense than living under the crushing weight of debt.

We left Jackson and moved to Paris, Texas, with the idea that we would "do the farm life" with the family. And we were able to do this for quite a while. We saved to purchase the farm and the house that fit our family's needs. I didn't work inhumane hours. I spent more time home on weekends and holidays. We were able to live on the farm that we dreamed of. But God had another spiritual truth to reveal to us. We were living in the country about twenty minutes outside of Paris. Many of the people in our community were not well off. Through our friendships with them, Laurie and I began to understand the curse of poverty.

It was there that we helped start a medical clinic for the indigent in Paris with a group of servant-hearted people. This

clinic was held at a local church as a service for the unin-
sured poor in our area. We offered clinical and even surgical
services through this program. I remember one case clearly:
a man came into the clinic one day with a hernia. This man
wasn't able to pass a work physical with a hernia, so he couldn't
get the money he needed for the surgery—meaning the hernia
was not getting repaired and he was not able to work. This type
of cycle can impoverish anyone very quickly. So I fixed the
hernia pro bono and petitioned the hospital to decrease their
bill so that the guy could get back to work. Everyone I worked
with at that clinic found similar ways of helping people.

During these years we also learned about God's heart for
unity. At the time, the Paris community was very divided—
people of different races were at odds, the hospitals were
arguing, and the churches didn't want to work together.
However, I felt deep in my heart that the Lord wanted Laurie
and me to be a force of unification. We were quite unsure how
to accomplish any act of unity. We knew what it was like to be
a part of strife and separation. It's easy to be a part of division.
How in the world could the two of us do anything that could
be helpful toward unity? We mustered our courage and invited
all of our friends over to our house for an evening of worship.
We intentionally invited folks from as many different denom-
inations as possible. Much to our surprise, folks came. They
endured our simple attempts to lead worship and, gratefully,
the chief of police was a talented musician who made us sound
much better than we actually were. Hebrews 13 talks about
Jesus suffering outside of the camp to give us sanctification. In
verse 13 it says, "Therefore let us go to Him outside the camp
and bear the reproach He endured." We lived in the country,
so we were offering a place where people could go "outside

of the camp" to encounter Jesus. One Saturday evening a month we would move the furniture out of our den and folks from all different backgrounds came to worship. Methodists, Baptists, agnostics, Catholics, blacks, whites, Hispanics—all were welcome. Worship lasted for hours. We saw people healed during this time of unity. We did that for many years, and we felt it reflected God's heart for unifying people across socio-economic and racial boundaries to come together to worship God and love one another.

We also felt called to join and support an interracial church. We met in a 1920s-era storefront right on the town square, which was a perfect location to minister to folks who were in need. Everyone there knew that nice clothing was not required to attend services and sometimes we would have folks still hungover from the night before sprawled across the sidewalk as we came in. We'd invite them into the building and give them some coffee hoping to sober them up enough to know that they were in church. This was a new way for us to do church. We were accustomed to getting dressed up to go to church; now, we were inviting drunks and prostitutes into our church and providing for their physical and spiritual needs. It was challenging but amazingly invigorating at the same time. It was lifechanging for us to enter a world that was outside our comfort zone and share life with people who were struggling just to get by. We were doing our best to answer God's call to work for unity in a divided community. We made lots of mistakes. We were often misunderstood, and there are many things I would do differently now if I had the chance, but there was a harvest of good fruit with many lives changed and many people brought into the Kingdom of God. Also through these days, the Lord was teaching us and preparing us for our time in Haiti. One humorous story that came from this church centered around Laurie as she served as the teacher for Ladies' Bible Class. Many of the ladies who came to this Bible study were former prostitutes as well as not-so-former prostitutes. One evening, the Bible study was about the book of Joshua. Rahab the harlot plays a pivotal role in the early part of the book. The discussion of a harlot led to talk about prostitution, which led to talk about how much money different women charge for their services. A fist fight actually broke out during the discussion when one woman felt the other women were insulting her for setting her prices too high. Laurie came home that night anxious to tell me about what had to have been one of the most unique conversations during any Ladies' Bible Class.

After five years in Paris, the Lord guided us to move to the Nashville, Tennesse, area. We had no idea why the Lord would call us there, and we were reluctant to leave Paris, but we wanted to be obedient. We rented a home while we searched for a house to buy. Months before we moved to Nashville, the Lord had given Laurie an unusual vision that our house would be in "fox hall," and she had seen in her mind's eye that one would have to cross a bridge over a stream in order to get to the front door. Neither one of us knew what this vision meant. We had a real estate agent who was pushing us to buy the type of house she usually showed to other doctors but none were anywhere near the budget we wanted to keep. We eventually convinced her that we would only look at smaller homes and one day, I just started driving around, looking on my own. I was by myself on one of these drives when I came across a home with a

"For Sale" sign in the front yard of the house. I pulled up and asked the mean there to tell me about the house. He told me that the house was in the neighborhood called Foxland Hall and then asked if I wanted to see inside. As I approached, I noticed that a fountain brook ran under a small bridge, right in front of the door. I immediately called Laurie.

So there we were, in a nice house in a comfortable neighborhood in Brentwood, Tennessee, still scratching our heads as to what the Lord had for us. We couldn't figure out why the Lord would move us back into a traditional lifestyle. We had given up near-sustainability on a farm in Paris to live in the Nashville suburb of Brentwood. I have to admit that this was a lifestyle of almost constant temptation. The call to success and comfort and the aura of prestige were the voices that I almost constantly heard. I tried to live a life reflective of Jesus, but the lure of the world was constant. I was very concerned that I had misunderstood the Lord and had even regressed in my faith. Time and time again I wondered, *Is this really the life You would have me lead?* It would take me several years before I found the answer to this question.

One morning I was sitting in the den of our Brentwood home near a window overlooking our side yard where deer and turkeys strutted around. I was cherishing the quiet of the morning when I picked up my Bible during one of my regular morning Bible studies and was shocked to feel as if I was hearing these familiar words for the very first time:

Is not this the fast that I choose:
to loose the bonds of wickedness,
to undo the straps of the yoke,
to let the oppressed go free,
and to break every yoke?
Is it not to share your bread with the hungry
and bring the homeless poor into your house;
when you see the naked, to cover him,
and not to hide yourself from your own flesh?
Then shall your light break forth like the dawn,
and your healing shall spring up speedily;
your righteousness shall go before you;
the glory of the Lord shall be your rear guard. (Isaiah 58:6–8)

As I read this passage, I saw the stark contrast between my current definition of success and what the Lord declared as His. I felt sick. I realized how I had been living for my own pleasure while I gave lip service to God. I wanted His blessing without sacrifice. I wanted comfort for myself more than I wanted it for others. I wanted to orchestrate my life in a way that insulated me from oppression. I was happy to deal with disease as long as it was in a sterile operating room. I would serve the poor as long as I could go home and sleep in my clean, temperature-controlled bedroom.

But that's not what this verse is saying. It says to share your bread, not just give access to bread. That means both the sharer and the receiver have less because they are both eating the portion meant for one. When it talks about bringing the homeless poor into your house, that doesn't exactly mean to build a homeless shelter—although I think that's good too. It means to allow them into your own personal space, and, more importantly, into your life. It isn't just an activity; there is a sacrifice involved.

Due to Laurie's kindness we allowed a woman, homeless and strung out on drugs, to stay with us for a time. She slept in our house and ate at our table with our kids. This was not what most would consider a safe thing. We had no idea how she would interact with our children. Bringing the homeless into your house is messy. Your carpets are no longer clean, your car no longer has that "new car smell." You share their troubles because they are facing you every day. You may end up using your own clothes to cover their nakedness as the verse suggests. And when you take your own clothes off to cover another, you are revealing some of yourself to the person you are covering. When that happens, it unifies you with the poor. And what comes through that is a tremendous blessing: "Then shall your life break forth like the dawn and your healing shall spring up speedily." But there is no shortcut to this—it requires sacrifice.

This passage makes it clear that we please God when we serve the hungry, the poor, and the naked. I studied fervently, flipping pages and looking up verse after verse, trying to read all of the ways to please God. I was able to grab onto the idea that sharing my bread and bringing the homeless into my home were the ways I could bring pleasure to God. I loved His imagery of my light shining like the dawn. As a doctor, I know the importance of healing, and this passage had a promise that my own healing would spring up speedily when I serve the poor. But what in me needed healing? It didn't take much soul-searching to realize the answer was that I needed healing for my arrogance, entitlement, and feelings of superiority that came from my wealth and level of education.

I needed to know God's definition of success. What I found unsettled me. His description of success is very different from the definition the world gives. *According to God, success is defined by our sacrifice.*

Now that's not a topic you'll see in any wealth management seminar. Oh, we may imagine that we can achieve financial success if we're willing to sacrifice sleep, free time, and sometimes our families. In surgery residency, I certainly believed that the more successful surgeons were those willing to sacrifice family time for time in the operating room. But God's definition of success *is* sacrifice. You give. You die. You become a servant. This is not the world's view of a successful life, but it is God's.

Even those of us in the church are not immune to the temptation of striving for worldly success. We dream of living in fine houses. We focus on comfortable furnishings. We pursue endless hours of entertainment. And though many of us donate to our church and various ministries, compared to what we spend on our houses, our cars, our vacations, and our children, our priorities don't seem aligned with God's priorities.

So how could I as a 21st-century American pursue God's definition of success? How could someone like me who lived in an affluent culture share God's vision? How could someone who's been primed for worldly success their entire life resist society's definition of success and believe in the contrarian notion of the success of *sacrifice*?

One day, I read a story.

Long ago there was a prosperous city whose citizens pursued success, and they were good at it. They were able to build an economic engine that fueled expansion at a fabulous rate. Businesses flourished, and food was abundant. They had all they needed and more.

Unlike other cities around them that struggled for survival, the citizens of this metropolis were able to take days off from work and enjoy vacations in luxury. They dressed in the latest fashions and expanded their houses and their land. They focused on comfort. They rested on comfortable beds, their chairs were overstuffed, and they walked in the most comfortable shoes of the day. They frequented spas where warm mineral water caressed their smooth skin and masseuses loosened their tight muscles.

The citizens of this city were a successful lot, envied by all who lived around them. They lived in lovely homes and dined on sumptuous fare. They were proud of their accomplishments and felt entitled to all the luxurious benefits of their culture.

Do these people sound like anyone you know?

Surprisingly, they're not the current residents of the Hamptons or Beverly Hills. In fact, the city described here is an ancient one, an infamous urban oasis usually remembered more for its destruction than its amazing achievements. The city is Sodom—the same Sodom that God destroyed along with Gomorrah.

"For behold, this was the guilt of your sister Sodom: she and her daughters had pride, excess food, and prosperous ease, but did not aid the poor and needy. They were haughty and did an abomination before me. So I removed them, when I saw it" (Ezekiel 16:49–50).

This passage is shocking to me. Do you see why Sodom was destroyed? It was obliterated because the people were proud, had excess food, and focused on their comfort and ease. And in the midst of their luxury, they did not take care of the poor and the needy. The people of Sodom were destroyed for what we might think of as innocuous things.

These are not what most people think of as damnable sins. We live in a culture that doesn't disdain pride. We're accustomed to having plenty of food on our plates. We admire people who live in luxury. And we often do this with little regard for the poor. The story of Sodom shows God's condemnation of the worldly definition of success.

In many ways, I felt that I related more to the description of the citizens of Sodom in Ezekiel 16 than I did to the picture of a people pleasing to God in Isaiah 58.

As an American, this worries me. It's hard to deny the similarities between our current culture and that of Sodom. We are considered by much of the world to be proud and arrogant. We show off our riches and our national strength at every turn, and we never seem to tire of showing our dominance. We can't deny our pride.

As for excess food, citizens of the United States are one of the most overweight on the planet. Close to 35 percent of us are obese, and the problem is only worsening. If we include those who are overweight, the percentage rises to 69 percent. The continent of Africa has a population *three times greater* than that of the United States. Yet the United States throws away more food every year than the continent of Africa consumes. If that isn't illustrative of our glut, I'm not sure what is.

And yet, for all our wealth, we spend a tiny percentage helping the poor. The average churchgoing American Christian only gives 2.5 to 3 percent of his income to charity. The average American atheist donates 2.5 percent to charitable causes. Simply put, we are not as generous as we could be, nor as we *should* be.

Jesus was known for His compassion because He fed the hungry, gave water to the thirsty, and healed the sick.

Here's something else to think about: If every churchgoing American Christian gave a full 10 percent of his income as a tithe to the Lord, and all that money was spent on food for the hungry, there would be no starving people left in the world.

None.

And yet our clamor for success drowns out the cries of the starving.

Can you imagine if we defined success by how many people we fed rather than by the building where we attend church?

Can you imagine the worldwide impact that we would have as Christians if we were known for providing food for the hungry, clean water for the thirsty, or medicines for the sick instead of our current reputation of what we are against?

Please don't misunderstand my point here. I am not saying that success is a bad thing or that we should not pursue it at all. We should absolutely pursue success. Jesus came to bring us a life of abundant joy, peace, and purpose. God delights in bestowing good gifts on His children and surprising them with His many blessings.

Success is not the problem; it's how we define it.

God's version of success is not found in pursuing and attaining worldly riches.

God's definition of success is a life of sacrifice that brings abundant life to others. This is stated in Romans 12:1: "I appeal to you therefore, brothers, by the mercies of God, to present your bodies as a living sacrifice, holy and acceptable to God, which is your spiritual worship."

Isn't this the description of Jesus's life? Didn't His life of sacrifice bring us abundant life?

I knew the Scripture reading: "[Jesus] came that [we] might have life and have it abundantly," (John 10:10). When I read this passage, I imagined the abundant life as being a comfortable home, healthy children, a loving spouse, and plenty of money. I failed to realize that Jesus's thirty-three years on earth are the perfect depiction of the abundant life. I wanted to reject His lifestyle of homelessness, poverty, and suffering and instead pursue wealth, prestige, and comfort. Jesus lived the abundant life. His life of sacrifice was actually the life of abundance.

How had my definition of abundant life become so anti-thetical to His? I had to ask myself, *Why do I pursue the pleasures of the world instead of pursuing His lifestyle?*

The life that God was calling me to was one of a living sacrifice. Just as Jesus sacrificed Himself on the cross so that I might live and live life abundantly, I am called to sacrifice myself so that others can live and experience abundant life. As I finally started to get a grip on the truth of His plan for my life, He showed me a mystery: *A life of sacrifice is an abundant life. The life of sacrifice also produces abundant life in others.*

Sacrifice is a learned trait that doesn't come all that natu-rally to us. We must be trained in sacrifice. If we never learn to sacrifice then we will be spoiled and unhappy people. As small children, we learn to sacrifice possession of our toys in order to make friends. As teens, we sacrifice our free time in order to play on a sports team. As parents, we sacrifice our time, energy, money, and sometimes even our careers in order to raise our children. At this point in my life, I felt God's call to specifically sacrifice the material comforts I had here in the States in order to minister to the poor abroad. I was called to give up what I most wanted to keep—financial success, material comfort, professional acclaim—in order to follow God's calling to help the poor.

No one can tell you what or how God will ask you to sacrifice in order to fulfill His calling on your life; that only comes from Him. But I can relate some stories that blessed my life of amazing friends and mentors who have sacrificed greatly and received an abundance of life that is truly amazing

The parents of one of my good friends were missionaries in East Asia. They had been called to a previously unreached tribe which had had little if any interaction with outsiders. As their little missionary group consisting of several young families began to attempt to minister the Gospel to this group, they were met by encouraging initial success. They began sharing gifts with the women of the tribe and seemed to be developing good relationships. One such meeting between the missionary men and the men of the tribe, however, resulted in the murder of the male missionaries. Although grieving for her husband, the mother of my friend stayed and continued to minister to the tribe whose member had killed her husband. Her work eventually led to an outpouring of grief and repentance by the responsible tribal members and has resulted in many of them accepting Jesus as their Lord and Savior as well as the establishment of a robust church there. Her incredible sacrifice opened the door for many to enter the Kingdom.

Another friend, Heidi Baker, is a missionary to the poor of Mozambique in southeastern Africa. She is an incredibly gifted woman who speaks nine languages and has a Ph.D. from King's College in London. She could be successful in almost any other endeavor, yet she chose to live in one of the poorest countries and devote her life to helping the poor. She has been assaulted and attacked many times, but she continues to be a light in Mozambique and around the world in the name of Jesus.

My dear friend Asher Intrater is a leader of the Messianic Jewish movement in Jerusalem. After graduation from Harvard, he sought for God through Central America and one day found Jesus and His saving grace in a rural chapel. He left the promise of a prosperous career in the United States for the uncertainty of serving the Jewish believers in Jesus in Israel. His family faces persecution daily. He tells of how one of his children was injured when people threw rocks at him for being a believer in Jesus. It is obvious that it hurts him that his faith had led to the injury of his son, but this hasn't stopped his ministry. Today, he stands as one of the most respected scholars in Israel and is seeing many come to the Lord in the Land of Israel.

Roberta Edwards went to Haiti in 1995 on a mission trip and saw the incredible need among the street children of Port-au-Prince. She moved permanently to Haiti soon after and founded a home for unwanted children. She made sure that her children were well fed, well-educated, and immersed in the love of Jesus. We became friends in 2013 and shared many stories and sweet times together. She was a dear source of encouragement to us. She endured the constant violence of Port-au-Prince with untrammeled grace until one day in 2015 she was murdered while sheltering her children from violence. She sacrificed everything for her 20 adopted children at the Sonlight Children's Home. I met with her several months before she died and was amazed by her tenacity for life and her persistent care for others through her orphanage and nutrition center. I'm reminded of Roberta each time I smell the flowers of the plumeria tree that we planted in her memory in our yard in Haiti.

These friends sacrificed prosperity, comfort, and their lives in order to pursue their passion for the Kingdom and by doing so, they lived life to its fullest. There are countless others who have sacrificed their worldly views of success to pursue God's calling in their lives and to realize the abundant life that results from such a sacrifice.

I wondered if I could follow in the grace-filled footsteps of these giants of the faith. I worried that I would fall short of the calling on my life. I needed more faith.

We finally realized that the Lord had placed us in Brentwood to continue the ministry of reconciliation and unity that we had learned in Paris and present it to people in the church who had the means to carry out a ministry to the poor through the nonprofit organization we would soon start. He used what we knew about poverty to help connect good people with compassionate hearts and open hands with ministry to the poor. It's all very clear to me now, but it took thirteen years of living there to figure it out. We didn't make this connection when we first began the organization as a response to Hurricane Katrina in 2005. It still wasn't clear when we were traveling to Honduras and Mozambique to offer medical assistance to local people. We didn't make the connection until we started leading teams of medical personnel to Haiti and Ghana.. The Lord allowed us to help make connections. He used our years in Brentwood as a time to prepare us for our coming sacrifices.

What could God be calling you to sacrifice next?

CHAPTER 6

ARROWS IN
THE QUIVER

*To live beyond means raising or mentoring
children who will carry the faith into the next
generation and beyond your own lifetime.*

MY FIRST SIX YEARS OF MARRIAGE WITH LAURIE WERE A BLESSED time. Though we had dated for seven years prior to getting married, this early time as husband and wife knitted us together and allowed us to understand the calling that God had on our lives more fully as a couple. During that time, we tried to establish traditions that would serve our family through the years. We began studying the Bible together regularly, seeking God's guidance on Scripture and trying to assimilate it into our lives. We prayed together. Praying with Laurie catalyzed our relationship in a way that is indescribable. Hearing her sincerely seeking the Lord's face and intently listening to His voice was pivotal in deepening both our relationship with each other and my relationship with the Lord. We tried implementing a ten-minute rule, that is, not to discuss difficult things within ten minutes of coming home from work. Instead, we just enjoyed each other's company to strengthen our marriage. Sometimes we succeeded, sometimes we didn't. We still struggle with that one! We also tried to never let the day end in a fight, also with varying success. We knew that the enemy exploited us by going to bed upset with each other, but it was hard for us to break that cycle.

We started a tradition of serving the poor. We knew the Scriptures about God's love and mercy for the less fortunate. "Whoever is kind to the poor lends to the Lord and He will repay him for his deed." (Proverbs 19:17) And, "But if anyone has the world's goods and sees his brother in need, yet closes his heart against him, how does God s love abide in him?" (1 John 3:17) As we wondered what that might look like in our lives, we began serving in homeless shelters and working in indigent medical clinics. I think it was on a cold Thanksgiving morning under the bridge in downtown Dallas serving meals to the homeless people of the area that I felt that we were possibly called to serve the poor long-term.

———

We were blessed with three wonderful children. Laurie and I always wanted a big family with lots of kids so that they would grow up understanding the importance of how a family can work together for a greater good. We decided early on to raise our children in a non-child-centric household. We wanted them to be others-centric. So on weekends, instead of driving from one ball field to another, they worked with us at the indigent medical clinic in Paris, Texas. They weren't there to play—they had jobs to do. On Saturdays they would check patients into the clinic, bring them water and food, and make sure they were seen by the medical staff as quickly as possible. Don't get me wrong, our kids had plenty of time for play and sports and music during the week. We just wanted them to experience the transforming power of serving others in Jesus's name first-hand on a regular basis—we made these weekends that time.

We wanted our children to realize that God had blessed us not so that we could accumulate more stuff but in order for us to bless other people, especially those in need. We wanted our children to understand that faith has to look like something. Living in the Bible Belt of America, we are accustomed to hearing and saying faith-filled expressions. But there is a world of difference between *sounding* like we have faith and *acting* upon our faith.

We live in a day when "works" are criticized. Many in Christian circles warn against "works-oriented Christianity," but we have raised our children to know that faith without works is not faith. Talk only produces hot air unless there is action to back it up.

You must understand—I am not talking about works-oriented salvation. There is only one way we are saved. We are saved by grace through faith, which is a gift of God (Ephesians 2:8–9). We cannot earn our salvation. Salvation is free, a gift. The only way to salvation is to receive this gift of grace through faith.

However, I am talking about works-oriented *faith*. I'm talking about what you do once you are saved. I'm talking about what you do *after* you've received the gift of salvation. How you live the Christian life. How you walk the walk, not just talk the talk. The Bible teaches us that faith without works is dead (James 2:17). We also believe that without faith, it's impossible to please God (Hebrews 11:6). Knowing those two things makes it pretty clear that we must live out our faith by doing the works God has called us to do: a works-oriented faith.

So what does this faith look like? Faith looks like spending less on yourself so that you have more money to give away. Faith looks like giving up a fancy meal or two so that someone else can have enough food to survive the month. Faith looks like sacrifice. Over the years, Laurie and I have had to learn the importance of this sacrifice. This wasn't something we fully grasped when we lived in Jackson or even Paris, but by the time we made it to Brentwood, we chose the less-flashy and more functional house over the larger ones that were at our disposal so that we had more funds available to give. We still fail miserably—but the conscious effort is putting us on the right track.

As parents, we are called to be the leaders of our family, so we led the children to participate in what we did—they were partners in whatever the family was doing. So when we started working in the mission field overseas as a family, it was completely natural for them to accompany us even though they were very young. The time together overseas wasn't abnormal or strange to them. It followed the natural progression of service—medical services in their hometown to medical services abroad. It was just what we did, and it did change our children's perspectives on life.

I remember one time in Mozambique, our youngest child, Jacklyn, was about 12 years old and had made friends with a girl in one of the villages we visited. Even though they didn't speak the same language, they communicated with each other as only young girls can. Because of chronic malnutrition, the little Mozambican girl was only about half Jacklyn's height, and she automatically assumed that Jacklyn was much older. (To be fair, Jacklyn was and still is fairly tall.) As their communications improved, they were quite shocked to learn they were the same age. It was unsettling for a 12-year-old American girl to come face to face with someone who was starving. The life to which we were accustomed didn't include hunger and deprivation. I know that this experience reoriented Jacklyn's thinking about the world we live in—that for many people life isn't made up of abundant food and entertainment or smooth roads and vacations but rather, hunger, dirty drinking water, and little access to medical care. But nothing prepared her for the horrors of her return visit the next year.

During our time in Mozambique, we worked to strengthen the existing medical infrastructure and understand the culture more fully. As an American, it's easy for me to believe that my culture is pervasive or dominant throughout the world, and it takes jarring circumstances to disrupt my faulty thinking.

As we prepared to return to Mozambique as a family, we all looked forward to seeing the friends we'd met on our previous trips. Jacklyn, in particular, looked forward to seeing the little girl she'd befriended and find out how she'd been doing since we'd last visited her village. The trip to Mozambique is somewhat arduous, and after the thirty-three-hour transit time, we were more than glad to arrive safely at our destination. After a short rest, we all went out to get reacquainted with the locals, and Jacklyn went to find her friend. When Jacklyn returned with the girl, I could tell that something was wrong. The little girl's countenance had changed. She was morose and looked as though she'd been crying. One of the locals explained to us that the custom in this area for the right of passage of young girls into womanhood was for the fathers to lock them outside their family hut at night and allow them to be abused by the elders of the village. This formerly bouncy little 13-year-old was now just a shell of her former self. While Jacklyn's year had been spent going to classes at school, going to sleepovers, and running track, this little girl had been brutalized.

How could one so young deal with such barbarity? As Jacklyn worked through the challenges of the reality of life for her friend, this event would become part of the focus of her life. She knew that her calling was to bring the love of Jesus to the oppressed. Now in her mid-twenties, Jacklyn has lived out her calling on a daily basis as a missionary to the Haitian people, specifically caring for girls and women.

As the youngest child and the only girl, Jacklyn did and still does receive preferential treatment. Our daddy/daughter bond is tight. The boys used to complain about it, but deep down they knew she was really special too. She was born during one of the biggest ice storms that West Tennessee had ever had, so none of our extended family was able to come to her birth. The quiet calm of having only our nuclear family there to welcome Jacklyn into the world was idyllic and set the tone for her early childhood.

Our family enjoys our traditions, and one of the most enjoyable involved just Jacklyn and me. From the age of just a few months old through high school, she and I would go on a weekly date. Of course, at first she just cooed in her bassinet, but as time went on our dates were filled with her descriptions of her hopes, dreams, successes, and heartaches. It was on those dates that we forged a bond that has lasted the years. As I write these words, she has recently forged new bonds with a different man, her husband, Connor. This special young man is an answer to our prayers. He's the type of man any father would be thrilled to have marry his daughter. Like Jacklyn, he has a heart for international evangelism, which is enabled by his job as an engineer with an international industrial gas supplier. They began their marriage living overseas and antic-ipate the many different countries where the Lord will allow them to work for His good. Connor loves the Lord with all his heart, and he demonstrates this through his love for Jacklyn. That's something that makes a doting dad's heart very happy.

Laurie and I were always very involved with our chil-dren's education. When they were small, we even home-schooled them for a while. Laurie is a great teacher, and at her feet, the children learned the great treasures that abound in history, English literature, and geography. She, of course, did the real work, but I would come in periodically and teach them science. One time, during a section on the anatomy of the heart, I saw an opportunity to be especially creative. A quick trip to the local slaughterhouse produced three cow hearts and a side trip to my office supplied us with scalpels and suture—all we needed to learn how to perform heart surgery. Around a table in the backyard, we dissected ventricles, excised valves, and sutured bypass grafts into coronary arteries. It was loads of fun, and the kids remember the lesson to this day, but the funny part came two days later at church. Jacklyn's Sunday School teacher was not a fan of homeschooling, and she voiced her reticence to us anytime she saw an opportunity. One such opening came as I picked five-year-old Jacklyn up at the end of her Sunday School. The teacher pulled me aside and said that she thought Jacklyn was lying. This came as quite a shock since Jacklyn was typically a truthful little girl, so I asked her to explain. She said that upon asking Jacklyn what she was learning in her homeschool classes, she proudly responded that we had been learning how to perform coronary artery bypass grafting. After waiting a beat for the effect, I responded in a shocked voice, "You mean your children aren't learning how to do heart surgery?" That promptly ended any further aspersions regarding our choice of education.

When she was little, Jacklyn was always the one who wanted to help me work on the car and later was the one who could always be depended upon to help me fix the generator in the middle of the night in Haiti, holding the flashlight for me until we restored power to our base. Many nights we would be roused from a deep sleep by the deafening silence that only comes from an electrical failure. On those many occasions, she would gladly get up and keep me company as we struggled in the dark to get our tired, old generator engine to start back up. Even though getting up in the middle of the night is no fun, she made it an adventure and we bonded even further during these times. I will genuinely miss our 2 a.m. rendezvous as she goes on to greater things.

John Mark, our middle child, was named for Laurie's little brother, Johnny. Johnny was born with Down syndrome and was the delight of the family. Likewise, our John Mark quickly became the delight of everyone around him. A born leader and athlete, he made friends quickly and kept them for life. As a fierce competitor on the football field and basketball court, he won the respect of his teammates and maybe inspired a little fear in his opponents. I remember one time on the high school football field, John Mark tackled a receiver running at full speed. After the resounding hit, the boy let out a loud painful cry. As the de facto team doctor, I ran onto the field to find the boy's elbow badly dislocated. An orthopedic surgeon friend and I gently relocated the elbow and sent the boy and his concerned parents off to the area hospital.

We both enjoyed martial arts so when he was young, we signed up for Krav Maga, an Israeli martial art form that was much more martial than art. For several years, we spent evenings practicing at the local gym and learning the discipline of this fighting style. As we progressed and he grew bigger and packed a bigger punch, the challenge became avoiding any injuries that would sideline my surgical practice. Many times, much to Laurie's chagrin, we would bring home the adrenaline-fueled moves we had learned that night and tear up the living room in the process.

John Mark's toughness as a competitor is matched only by his self-discipline. When the children were young, we bought a farm in the rolling hills south of Nashville. This farm became a refuge for the family and a place for John Mark to prove his masculinity and fortitude. He chopped firewood, shredded pastures, hunted deer, and caught fish on this little piece of Middle Tennessee. John Mark loved to camp by the small river that ran through our place. He would often wait for the coldest day of the year, pack up his old Ford pickup, and head out to the farm. Once there, he would pitch his tent, light a fire with only one match, and proceed to catch his dinner. He might come home the next day a little cold, smelling of camp-fire smoke, and sometimes a bit hungry from an unsuccessful fishing trip, but he was always happy to have proven himself in this way. These long, cold nights of solitude in the impenetrable darkness of a Middle Tennessee winter night taught him a lot about toughness, about resilience, and about himself.

On January 12, 2010, John Mark's resilience was truly tested. As news of the earthquake in Haiti spread and the numbers of estimated dead rose, so did the shock and disbelief of the American people at the tragedy that had hit Haiti. We mobilized our small team to travel to Haiti and set up at a hospital. As we checked and rechecked our disaster relief kit, I knew that this upcoming experience was going to be a significant event in his life, challenging him in ways that even his personal tests couldn't match. As he went from patient to gravely injured patient setting bones and giving hope, I saw a snapshot of the strength and compassion that characterizes his adult life.

Through college he excelled academically as well as romantically, marrying Lauren, a beautiful Oklahoman who equally shares his love for the Lord. We had the honor of working with Lauren before they were married. She lived with us for six months before she started college and traveled to many of our mission sites throughout the world with us sharing her many skills with the poor and oppressed. During this time together, we grew to love and appreciate her more than ever.

John Mark and Lauren continued to serve with LiveBeyond for several years. She as mission trip coordinator and he in the role of systems coordinator. They both advanced the organization greatly by their individual unique qualifications. John Mark was part of our innovations lab, which studied and implemented new innovative solutions to ease poverty in the developing world. These systems have made major inroads into helping to solve the problems of the poor in the areas we touch.

Our eldest, David, was born during my first month of surgery residency. He was the third generation David Vanderpool born at Baylor University Medical Center. My dad, Brice David Vanderpool, was born there in 1932 and practiced surgery at that hospital for 50 years. In 1960, I was born there and completed five years of post-doctoral education there in surgery. Finally, David Stallings Vanderpool was born there in 1987. People took pictures and wrote articles, and then Laurie and I headed home with our beautiful, blue-eyed baby boy.

We lived in a small, three bedroom house with blue shutters and rocking chairs on the front porch on an idyllic cul-de-sac in the Lake Highlands area of Dallas, not far from where Laurie grew up. David was an absolutely wonderful baby. He laughed, he played, and he loved it when we read to him. In fact, I was convinced that by age 2 he'd memorized the books we read to him because if I skipped a page in an attempt to get him to bed earlier, he would insist that I go back and read it.

His early childhood was almost cut short when at age 6 he fell from his horse. His "mighty steed" was a Shetland pony named Lover, but when the girth broke and little David hit the ground, he ruptured his spleen. As a surgeon, I was shocked that my own son had suffered a potentially fatal injury, an injury that I'd taken care of many times in others. We rushed him to the area hospital where his spleen was removed, and his life saved. The scar on his little belly was quite impressive. I'm pretty sure he used it to impress his friends later on when he was in high school. In spite of his injury, he grew up excelling at football, wrestling, and track.

He and John Mark always slept in the same room and they bonded as only brothers can by sharing their young lives and adventures together. Their late-night talks about life, love, and the future set the course of their friendship, but it was the twilight discussions about their faith and relationship with Jesus that set the course of their lives. They grew up knowing the saving power of their Lord Jesus Christ, and they constantly looked for ways to implement their nascent faith.

Before they could drive, they started a neighborhood lawn care business. They would push the mower and carry their weed eaters around the neighborhood and knock on the doors of the houses with particularly overgrown lawns. Their first season was a success. With the addition of a newly minted driver's license and an old Ford pickup truck complete with a trailer, they had high hopes for the upcoming season. They cleaned their weed eaters, sharpened the blades, and changed the oil of their mower in anticipation of overflowing bank accounts. Their visions of Amazon-like success were eclipsed, however, by a seemingly insignificant deed.

Our neighbor, a golf professional, had been injured and required surgery. This put him out of commission for an extended period of time and kept him from mowing his previously fairway-perfect lawn. Seeing the neighbor's plight, David offered to mow his lawn without charge. Though the neighbor protested, David really didn't take no for an answer. As weeks went by, a relationship grew, and from the relationship came the opportunity for David to share his faith. Our neighbors had experienced a harmful rejection by their previous church and had turned away from their childhood faith. Their lives reflected their hurt, and they had not recovered. But David's cheerful demeanor disarmed them, and his weekly lawn care visits opened them up to hearing the Gospel. Through a simple act of kindness one summer, they saw Jesus in action in a sixteen-year-old boy. They subsequently gave their lives to the Lord and have been faithful to Him to this day.

After college and with a Bible degree in hand, David volunteered to move to Haiti full-time to run our operations there. After a year in Port-au-Prince, he moved out to Thomazeau and lived among the villagers. At 6' 4" and 250 pounds, he was twice the size of the average Haitian; he had not suffered from any nutritional deficiencies that stunted growth as many Haitians do. He quickly learned the language and won the hearts of the villagers with his big smile and kindness. As he walked through the villages at night, he would stop at their huts to talk and eat the occasional dinner with people. They christened him the "Gran Blan," the big white one, (not too far off from my nickname for him of "Big Un") and grew to love his affability and fearlessness.

Through his conversations with the people of the area, he realized that a key to relieving their incessant hunger was to teach them improved and appropriate agricultural techniques. Soon thereafter, he was admitted to Texas A&M University's College of Agriculture to pursue a master's degree in agricultural leadership and education.

One day my phone rang and the voice on the other end of the line said, "Dad, what do you think about me going to Afghanistan with the U.S. Army to teach the people how to improve their farming techniques?" After a short pause for a prayer for wisdom, I replied, "That sounds like a great opportunity!" I'm pretty sure that I was trying to convince myself with that statement. After qualifying with the M4 and M9 and receiving a barrage of vaccines, he was off to FOB Ghazni, Afghanistan. His days were spent in the fields of Ghazni province teaching the farmers better farming techniques to improve their nutritional status and that of their families. After ten long months he was finally home, thirty pounds of muscle heavier and armed with the godly calling to spread the Gospel to the poor by teaching them how to better feed themselves.

He married his college sweetheart, Devin, a beautiful girl from the Hill Country of Texas. She grew up in a wonderful God-fearing family as an athlete and scholar ironically close to the small town of Vanderpool, Texas. Her college years prepared her to speak into the lives of troubled youths as a teacher and in graduate school, she further sharpened her skills to that of a wordsmith. With a master's degrees in creative writing and publishing, she perfected her passion of furthering the Kingdom by the written word. Their year apart, separated by the brutal mountains of the Afghan Kush, strengthened their relationship and prepared them to serve the Lord in some of the harshest places on earth.

Off to an arid region of Haiti to teach improved farming techniques on the one hand and literacy on the other, the new couple showed the love of the Lord Jesus Christ to thousands and received many into the Kingdom. Their two years together in Haiti created an indelible mark on the hearts and minds of the people of Thomazeau who to this day love them dearly.

———

"Like arrows in the hands of a warrior are children born in one's youth. Blessed is the man whose quiver is full of them." (Psalm 127:3-4)

In August 2005, Hurricane Katrina devastated the Gulf Coast. I didn't even think twice about heading south to do whatever I could as a trauma surgeon for the thousands of people injured and suffering. While I was getting ready to go down to Mississippi, David told me he wanted to come. He was about eighteen, right at the beginning of football season of his senior year—a pretty big time in a kid's life—and nothing about school or practice or games even factored into his decision to help. He was ready to go. I knew that his muscles and stamina would be an enormous asset during the recovery effort. So as a warrior in the battle against poverty, I knew it was time to shoot one of the arrows God had blessed me with: my eldest son.

"Son," I said, "Pack your bags."

"Are you serious?" he asked. "Awesome!"

Driving south to Biloxi after Katrina proved to be every bit the adventure any teenage boy would hope it would be. We loaded up his old green pickup truck with a chainsaw to cut up fallen trees, some basic tools, and as many medical supplies as we could squeeze in. We only had to drive a few hours to discover country roads and state highways entirely swallowed by mud and debris.

A question I often heard in the aftermath of the storm was, "Why didn't more people evacuate when they knew the hurricane was coming? Since so many had lost their homes in past storms, why hadn't they moved to a safer location?"

Such questions emanate from a lack of understanding of what it means to be so impoverished that you can't afford to leave. Many Americans can't fathom that the people living along the Gulf Coast simply didn't have anywhere else to go. The questioners assume, based on their own life experiences, that those in Katrina's path could have gone to stay with friends or relatives elsewhere. They don't understand that many people had little to start off with and then lost everything.

Standing water, still waist-deep, had left entire communities submerged. Many people simply needed clean drinking water, food, dry clothes, and help finding their loved ones. Others needed basic medication that they customarily received by mail. Unfortunately, the postal service wasn't going to be delivering anytime soon. Some needed surgeries that were unavailable since many of the area hospitals had lost power. Despite the best efforts of the Red Cross, numerous churches and ministries, and state and federal agencies, it was difficult to bring any kind of immediate order to the chaotic aftermath of Katrina.

The Bay Vista Baptist Church served as a central hub for much of the relief efforts in their area and allowed us to use their building as a base of operations. For days, we worked alongside the Red Cross, providing medical care to those stranded by the storm. Driving through the back roads of Biloxi, we found many people in desperate need of medications and care. It didn't take long for us to exhaust the stockpile of supplies we had brought. We returned home to restock for another run.

After several trips back and forth, Laurie suggested we buy a trailer and outfit it as a mobile medical treatment facility. I made some calls, and soon we had a vehicle equipped to treat minor injuries. We were able to use this setup to see injured patients in a dry, sanitary environment.

One time, as David and I cruised the flooded streets of the Biloxi/Gulfport area looking for people in need, we came upon a crowd who began calling out to us. There was a man who needed medical attention. Three days earlier, he had been trying to move a fallen tree from his house in waist-deep water when an alligator bit him on the leg. Now he was in dire need of treatment. Because the local hospital's backup electrical systems were located below the waterline in the basement of the building, they had no power. We were able to stabilize him, debride his wounds, and dress them. We returned to his house twice a day to change his dressing until the post-hurricane tornados cleared sufficiently to allow a medical flight to take him to a trauma center. We praised God when we got word that his leg and his life were spared.

We ended up going to serve those devastated by Hurricane Katrina off-and-on for eighteen months, and God opened doors for us on every trip. On one of our trips, we pulled into a railroad station that had been converted to a clinic. We weren't sure if anyone was there, but David knocked on the door. The people inside were obviously upset. They had completely run out of supplies and were contemplating closing. Our shipment was exactly what they needed to continue their efforts in their community! We took several runs of supplies to that location throughout the rest of our relief efforts.

As word spread among our extended families, friends, colleagues, and church community, many people wanted to contribute whatever they could to our efforts—food, time, medical supplies, and money. We were overwhelmed by the outpouring of help. Due to the growing scale of our involvement, we decided to form a 501(c)(3) nonprofit organization, *Mobile Medical Disaster Relief*, the early name of *LiveBeyond*.

Laurie and I had always talked and dreamed about working full-time in the mission field, and we were suddenly catching small glimpses of what that might look like. We prayed often for our children. We hoped that spending time with the "least of these" when they were young would inspire them to use their talents to bless those who have so little. We prayed that they would fully realize that the real joy in life comes from serving. That they would know we don't live life to the fullest and give God the leftovers but that we give Him the best part of our lives and wealth. That their faith in Jesus Christ was honed and perfected by what they did for those who suffer from oppression.

I'm beyond honored that God blessed us with three powerful arrows in our quiver. So when the earthquake shook Haiti in 2010, I took two of my arrows: David and John Mark. At the time, David was twenty-two, a triathlete and a Bible major finishing up his senior year at Abilene Christian University. He was excited to get to work in ministry, and Haiti gave him that opportunity in spades. Meanwhile, John Mark was a senior in high school, contemplating life at Texas A&M University. Together we prepared to go into battle. But MMDR and the Vanderpool family did a lot of growing between Katrina and Haiti. Our next stop was Mozambique.

CHAPTER 7

BOLDLY PURSUING THE KINGDOM OF GOD

To live beyond means to risk everything
boldly pursuing the Kingdom of God.

JOSEPH OF ARIMATHEA WAS DESCRIBED AS "A RESPECTED MEMBER of the Council, who was also himself looking for the kingdom of God." (Mark 15:43) We remember him most for taking care of Jesus's body after His death on the cross. As a voting member of the Council, the Sanhedrin, he was a very important man in Israel. His reputation carried a certain weight that not many men were afforded. But he was one of the few to connect Jesus to the Kingdom of God because he was looking forward to that Kingdom. He went to Pilate and boldly asked for the body of Jesus, risking his reputation and even his life in opposition to those on the Sanhedrin who sent Jesus to the cross. He paid a heavy price to buy the fine linen and the tomb for Jesus. But that's what happens when you look forward to the Kingdom of God. You are bold. You pay any price required. You do things that others might consider a little out there. But your faithfulness is rewarded because things tend to happen.

There is a change that takes place in people when they are looking forward to or taking delight in the Kingdom of God. There is little risk being a Christian in the United States today. But historically, and today in other places around the world, pursuing the Kingdom involves huge risk. And many of us tend to shrink back from that risk. Many Christians today want following Jesus to look like the movie *It's a Wonderful Life*. In reality, it looks a little like *Indiana Jones*, but you get some great stories.

Shortly after we wrapped up our disaster relief efforts for Hurricane Katrina, I found myself on a trip to Israel with my mentor, evangelical pastor Don Finto and Nashville-area attorney David Hooper. This was not an MMDR trip, but I was scouting for a new place to work. We went to Cyprus, the island off of the coast of Lebanon, to visit a Messianic

Jewish missionary who ran a camp for Israeli Messianic Jews to rest and get away from the craziness of life in Israel. It was a peaceful refuge nestled away in the mountains. There we met some missionaries from Ukraine and the country of Georgia who asked if I'd ever heard of Heidi Baker. I hadn't. They said that I needed to watch one of the videos of her ministry. During the video, I learned about her work through international nonprofit IRIS Global in Mozambique, and I felt that the Lord was telling me that was where I should go next. I immediately began writing to her office in California but got no response. About six months later, our friend, the Messianic Rabbi, Asher Intrater, was staying at our house during the summer while he preached around Nashville. He came into the kitchen for breakfast one day and said he had gotten an email from a woman in Mozambique named Heidi asking him to come to teach on her mission base. Asher felt like the Lord wanted me to go with him. Asher didn't know that this was the organization I had been trying to contact to no avail. His invitation was an answer to my prayers. We went several times, and I ended up supplying and working in the Iris medical clinic.

Heidi and her husband, Roland, are two Christians dedicated to living out their faith. When Laurie and I were beginning to understand our place in the Kingdom, Heidi and Roland had already been mightily advancing the Kingdom for many years. Laurie and I both looked to Heidi and Roland as role models as we grew our ministry.

One of the projects I got to work on in Mozambique was a chicken project. The director of operations, who was named Don, wanted to start a chicken project in Mieze village to help combat starvation and to teach entrepreneurial skills. He had been training the village leaders for months on how to manage the chicken production. So we purchased about 100 baby chicks and dropped them off. The next day, we went back out to visit and found that they had eaten all of the chicks. They said they were so hungry they couldn't help it. And those chicks barely had a scrap of meat on their bones! We repeated this process a few more times until we got smart. To fill their hungry bellies, we held a feast for the village in celebration of the project before we gave them the chicks. That night a huge storm brought high winds and torrential rain. We just knew the chicks had drowned. The next morning, Don and I drove back through the mud to find that the chicks were miraculously still alive! We asked how the locals kept the chickens alive, and they told us that they stayed up all night shoveling water out of the coop and covering them with the tarps from their own houses. When they spoke about the chicks, they referred to them as "our chicks"—no longer "Don's chicks" or "Dave's chicks." They finally felt ownership of the project. We knew it would be a success.

A few trips later, Don told me that we needed to check on the project, so we went to Mieze again. The leaders were thrilled to tell us that a neighboring enemy village had asked *them* for help with a chicken project. The Mieze village leaders agreed to help them, and their work together resolved the issues between the two warring tribes! Peace was made through chickens.

The miraculous was constantly happening in Mozambique, evidence that the faithful were boldly pursuing the Kingdom of God. One group accompanied Don and the rest of his team to help distribute food in an area severely affected by malnutrition. They took enough chicken, beans, rice, and soft drinks for about 100 kids, but at least 200 showed up. As they were passing out the food, the team realized that they were going to run out. They started praying that the Lord would multiply what they brought, specifically the soft drinks because they knew how much had been accounted for. They kept passing out food and drinks, and to their great joy, found that they had enough for 200!

One of the missionaries in Pemba had started a sewing school for women to help them provide for their families. Women were treated harshly in this community. Many of the women in the community were raped and abused, left to care for their families alone. The average number of children they cared for was close to twelve because they would take in the children of any family member who died and often took pity on children left in the streets. The sewing school was a beacon of hope in a bleak situation, but they didn't have many points of distribution. We offered to be a distributor for them in the U.S. of their purse line called "Handbags of Hope." We packed suitcases full of the purses when we came back from Mozambique and sent money back when we returned.

On another trip I found myself bumping along in the passenger seat of a Land Rover down a dirt path to a Maconde village west of Pemba for evangelism and a mobile medical clinic. Our plan was to drive at night and be ready for the clinic the next morning. Heidi Baker was in the first car, and she is an excellent driver. She was keeping a good clip, but because it was nighttime and pitch-black outside, she didn't notice right away when our vehicle broke down. There were about fourteen of us crammed into a car headed to the middle of nowhere—and now we were stuck. All of the security alarms in my head were blaring that we were stranded, so I got out and immediately went to my cellphone—no service. I checked my satellite phone, but it wasn't working well either. We checked the vehicle, but it wasn't anything we could fix without the proper equipment. So with nothing else to do, we all circled up and prayed. As we finished the prayer and lifted our heads, we heard a large truck coming up the path behind us. This part of Mozambique is very hilly with large sand dunes, and we could hear the truck's gears grinding as it went up and down each hill. Eventually, we could even see its headlights, bouncing along wildly. We couldn't believe our eyes when a tilt-bed wrecker pulled up. There were three men in the wrecker: one South African man and two Mozambican men. All three were inebriated.

The South African asked, "Do you have problems with your Rover?"

We outlined the problem for him, and he told us that he could fix it in his shop. He asked if he could take it with him now and deliver it in the morning. Our group was stumped at this point. We had no clue where we were going or how we would get there without the truck, it wasn't our truck to begin with, and the only guy who could fix the vehicle was drunk.

About that time Heidi had found a place to turn around and made it back to us. She set everything up with the South African to have the Rover fixed and delivered to our village the next morning. We squeezed into Heidi's car (a small miracle in itself) and continued on our way. You can't get that kind of service in Highland Park, Dallas, but we got it in the middle of nowhere, Mozambique.

We continued our journey on to the Maconde village. Heidi had not been to this one before, and this Maconde tribe had a reputation for being very fierce. Historically, the Maconde people were able to resist falling prey to the slave trade while the Makua people were traded around the world. In this part of Mozambique, the Makua and the Maconde were enemies. It was well after midnight when we came upon a roadblock manned by people with AK47s. I listened as Heidi debated with them in their native tongue before she whispered to the group, "This isn't going well. You should prepare yourself." We were taken from the vehicle and put into a mud hut jail for the rest of the night. Our captors shot off their guns into the air and touched the hot muzzles to our skin. Our group began to sing praise hymns to God to keep our spirits up through the long night. At dawn, the chief of the area showed up and said that we would be set free if we would provide medical care for his wife and children. As this was our plan all along, we agreed and quickly set up our clinic. The native people wanted the medical care but were not interested in Jesus. Heidi found a way around the issue. She set up a projector and a huge white sheet near our medical clinic so that the patients interested in the clinic might stay for that night's showing of *The Jesus Film* in their native language. I had trepidation since the night before had not gone well, but the chief came to the Lord along with many other villagers. Heidi eventually built a church in that village. Heidi and her team boldly pursued the Kingdom of God in the face of great danger and imprisonment, and the reward was great.

On some of my trips to Mozambique, I was able to do some disaster relief work. The Zambezi River, which flows across the lower half of the country, tends to flood during the rainy season. In 2007, Category 4 Cyclone Favio caused the river to flow well out of its banks, leading to the evacuation of about 80,000 people. I was part of a team helping pull people out of the water. These teams had to have at least two people: one to offer assistance to anyone found stranded due to flooding and the other to act as a spotter for crocodiles. Nile crocodiles are the most dangerous crocodile species, resulting in the death of hundreds of people each year. They can outswim you, outrun you, and the really aggressive ones are the biggest—some nearly the size of a car. We all learned a lot about faith during that time!

There was a chemical spill in the water in which I was swimming at one point during our rescue efforts. We never found out what it was, but I still have the scars from the painful chemical burns on my legs. The 33-hour flight back to the United States was not the most comfortable flight I've ever been on, but after witnessing the faithfulness of those around me, I knew what it meant to risk life, and especially limb, to boldly pursue the Kingdom like Joseph of Arimathea. During our work in Mozambique, we began supplying clinics around the world and even built a clinic in Cedeño, Honduras, in 2009–2010. But the Lord was preparing Mobile Medical Disaster Relief (MMDR) for a battle, one that would test us beyond human strength and endurance, one that would allow us to boldly pursue the Kingdom of God beyond our wildest dreams. That battle was in Haiti.

CHAPTER 8

THE BATTLE

To live beyond means taking up arms against sin, suffering, and evil in all its many forms.

I CAUGHT A GLIMPSE OF THE BATTLE WE WERE FACING WHEN MY sons and I walked into the hospital after the earthquake in Haiti. I soon learned the Herculean efforts our patients had made to travel to our location. Some arrived on foot while friends and family carried some earthquake victims with shattered limbs as delicately as they could during the long march. Donkeys conveyed some injured survivors strapped to their backs. The riders grimaced and cried out in pain with each step the animals took. A few pickup trucks, each laden with twenty or so of those fortunate enough to get a ride, ground their gears up the hill to our emergency room. Hundreds had arrived ahead of us, eagerly awaiting the medical attention we were there to offer. We were drastically outnumbered, and they kept coming.

Thinking that *our* journey to get there had been grueling, our small team had all looked forward to a short respite before we started to work, but this was not to be. We quickly transformed the vacant spaces into operating rooms as the mass of injured humanity filled every spare inch of space. As we surveyed the carnage, the Lord blessed us with a new team member. Richard, a former Army Special Forces medic who was living in the Dominican Republic, arrived with a willing heart, ready to do what he could to help the injured.

My sons transported patients and did their best to help alleviate the suffering. John Mark brought me a three-month-old baby girl whose arm had been pinned beneath tons of rubble. Recognizing she had a shattered arm, my son desperately hoped I could reconstruct it. Examining this precious baby as she slid further into shock, I recognized the waning of what we refer to as the "golden hour" of trauma. During the first sixty minutes after a significant injury, appropriate care is crucial to the survival of the injured. It was obvious that the hour for this baby had passed, limiting her hope of survival.

It has always fascinated me how five years of grueling training in surgery residency can be singularly focused on the urgent needs of one patient. Despite the screams and cries from the hundreds of severely injured around us, I took my son's desperate plea to save her life as a special call from God, and we concentrated all our efforts on saving this little girl. Rapid resuscitation followed by definitive surgery brought a bittersweet end. The baby girl was saved at the great cost of her arm.

Throughout that night and nonstop for three more days, we set broken bones, stemmed hemorrhages, and amputated crushed limbs. There is no doubt in my mind that the Lord was our strength. The hours we worked were similar to those I worked during residency, but it had been a few years since then and I was no longer accustomed to that pace. Not even caffeine could have sustained the three of us as we worked hour upon hour. The only reasonable explanation is the Lord's kindness. I was proud of how tirelessly my boys both faced the grim situation in front of them. They saw the problems and were willing to do whatever they could, sacrificing themselves, to reach solutions. Many of the most severely injured didn't live to see the dawn, and the body count became overwhelming. The breeze carried the stench of death and seemed to bring more patients to our waiting room. Someone, probably a representative from the Dominican government, set up a morgue near the hospital. If the bodies weren't claimed within a certain time period, they had to be cremated for sanitation purposes.

Exhausted and numb, I felt I was losing the battle. Nonetheless, life-or-death moments repeatedly crystallized my focus. Though I couldn't understand her Creole language, I could tell one woman was begging me to save her life. Her eyes pierced me as they lost their focus and began to slip to the ubiquitous black of the dying. She had been trapped under slabs of concrete in a market in Port-au-Prince for hours before she was rescued. Her pelvis had taken the brunt of the force and was shattered beyond repair. Now, despite my best efforts, she continued to hemorrhage. Without lifesaving blood transfusions and specialized equipment, I was left with little else to do but wrap her hips tightly with a compressive bandage and pray.

As I was finishing, I heard the words, "Dad, she's dying." I looked up to see my son David running toward me carrying yet another trauma victim in his arms, an eight-year-old girl named Jovanica. As she dangled from his arms, I saw that her leg had been crushed.

When we loaded her onto a stretcher, I noticed that both of her parents were with her. I quickly explained to them that we had to amputate her leg to save her life. As any parents would be, they were reluctant.

"There must be another way, something else you could try," they begged.

"I'm sorry, there isn't," I said in broken Creole.

"But she's only a child," her mother sobbed.

"She'll die."

As Jovanica slipped into the inevitable coma that blood loss produces, they finally consented. The golden hour of trauma for this girl also was long past and the chances of her survival neared zero. She was far beyond the point of fighting death.

She had accepted it, but her parents hadn't. That heightened the tension in me to help her survive.

As we rushed her to the OR, her feeble pulse skipped, skipped again, then was gone. Frantically, we gave fluids and pumped on her tiny chest, praying that she would live as we pushed ahead with the cruel but life-saving surgery. The crushed tissues were pumping a toxic cocktail throughout her fragile body, and her heart didn't like it. As soon as the source of the poison was separated from her body, her heart responded.

She spent the next week in our ICU in and out of a coma, but she soon turned the corner and began to improve. Her father was a constant presence at her side and soon became her crutch. Our eyes welled with tears as she and her dad walked together throughout the compound arm in arm, using his leg as her temporary prosthesis.

Those first seventy-two hours in Haiti were like being on the front line of a battle. Blood was everywhere, shattered bones protruded through patients' skin, and the screams of those in agonizing pain echoed through the halls. Bereft of sleep, food, and adequate support, we struggled through with our small team until other volunteers arrived.

Many people in the States worked hard to get the word out and medical professionals responded in droves. By the end of that first week, other doctors, nurses, and much-needed supplies arrived in huge quantities, saving the lives of thousands of Haitians. True heroes, these tireless medical staff members, logistics experts, and church volunteers worked around the clock to bring healing and sustenance to the injured Haitians.

Near the end of that first week, several more doctors and nurses joined our ranks, including some fantastic orthopedists. I had to send the boys back to the States since they were still in school, but the new volunteers took over their duties and relieved me enough so I could grab a few hours of sleep every once in a while to help me keep my mind clear. As more medical staff and support personnel arrived, I began to accompany daily trips into Port-au-Prince to push through the rubble and bring the injured back to the hospital. Driving off-road took on a whole new meaning as we navigated jutting slabs of asphalt, broken concrete, boulders, and potholes. Clothing, debris, and animal carcasses littered the villages where entire neighborhoods had collapsed as the ground rumbled beneath them.

On one trip, we noticed two helicopters sitting in the outfield of a baseball park we frequently passed on our way to the border. Curious about their purpose and desperate for a better mode of transportation, we stopped to get more information. Behind a folding table under a large tent, three men dressed in black T-shirts and military-style pants sat watching us. As we approached them, I noticed, in addition to the helicopters, a large shipping container full of supplies, numerous satellite phones, and a large flatbed truck.

Because of their obvious excellent physical conditioning, sophisticated supplies, and field-agent style of dress, I assumed that they were members of the CIA or some other covert three-letter government agency. I inquired about the helicopters and they agreed to help transport us to and from Port-au-Prince to provide care for the injured. Thinking that they were in a generous mood, I asked to borrow the flatbed truck. When they agreed again, I just knew that they had to be some kind of government operatives.

This idea was shattered, however, when they saw my satellite phone on my belt and asked, "You know how to use that phone?"

"Sure," I said. "Satphones are a necessity down here."

"Can you show us how to use one?" they asked, looking a little sheepish and pointing toward the half-dozen satphones I'd noticed.

I agreed and couldn't resist satisfying my curiosity. "Uh, guys, you're obviously from the States, right? Are you part of a government agency or ...?"

They began to chuckle. As we got better acquainted, they told us that they were a group of men from the Mormon church who had made a lot of money in their businesses and were there just trying to help. But once they arrived, they weren't sure how best to utilize the many resources they had brought. We became friends and worked together throughout our stay.

———

Remember the eight-year-old girl whose leg we had to amputate? About a year later, during one of our monthly trips to Haiti, David and I walked up to the front of a church on a Sunday morning and saw two familiar figures. A tall man balanced a one-legged, nine-year-old girl against his hip on the steps of the church. I would have known that man and girl anywhere. This was Jovanica, the same girl on whom we had operated and prayed over the year before. Her father had stayed with us long after her surgery, working as an orderly for us because he was so thankful that his daughter survived. The pair had heard that we were visiting the church that day, and they traveled a long way on several tap-taps (the Haitian taxi system) to visit us. I imagine their long voyage came with a significant cost as well. Most of the victims we worked on that day basically disappeared. We never saw them again. But it was amazing to get to see one of the patients we had worked so tirelessly to save. After hugs were exchanged and tears were dried, they recounted her time after leaving the hospital and the struggles she had endured that year with only one leg.

Jovanica lived close to the epicenter of the earthquake, and the uneven, rocky streets had proven too much for her. She had withdrawn from school because the children made fun of her and she couldn't walk that far unaided. She couldn't help her mother get water like the other girls in the village could either. With nothing left to tie her to her community, she had become reserved and shy. Fortunately, we had recently partnered with a group that fabricated prostheses for the earthquake victims. After a few simple measurements, we parted, she with the promise of mobility and I with a very full heart.

The battle for life since the earthquake in Haiti began with rescue and recovery, with agonizing choices, blood and suffering, and the concerted efforts of both people on the ground and people sending money, food, and supplies from far away. That battle continues though now on different fronts. Battles to feed the hungry. Battles to educate the children and find homes for the orphans and provide limbs to the amputees. Battles to create businesses and livelihoods that will enable the Haitian people to support themselves and their families. And battles to address the unjust systems, political corruption, and sheer prejudice that impede the Haitian nation. These battles don't seem as urgent to most, but they are just as deadly. God cares deeply about the oppressed. "The Lord is near to the brokenhearted and saves the crushed in spirit." (Psalm 34:18) "Whoever oppresses a poor man insults his Maker, but he who is generous to the needy honors Him." (Proverbs 14:31) And He encourages us to get involved when we see oppression. "Learn to do good; seek justice, correct oppression; bring justice to the fatherless, plead the widow's cause." (Isaiah 1:17)

In my work in Haiti, I've been privileged to meet many warriors, people who live beyond in order to battle sin, suffering, and every form of evil. They sacrifice their lives to fight the battles of injustice. Mission of Hope has worked for over thirty-five years battling against disease, starvation, and the oppression caused by a lack of education. For almost twenty years, Hope for Haiti's Children has cared for orphaned children and offered leadership opportunities to Haiti's youth. Immediately following the earthquake, I had the privilege of working with a Turkish and an Israeli disaster relief group. They were organized and more than willing to donate equipment to our mission to save lives.

And then there are the Haitian people themselves. They are not just passive victims, waiting for someone to rescue them. We met John Kely Garçon at a refugee center in Port-au-Prince. He was serving tirelessly as a translator, helping anyone and everyone he could find. We reconnected with him later and he became our Haitian base manager. He is now in the "great cloud of witnesses" since he gave his life for the Kingdom of God in the ultimate way. In 2017, while on his way to the LiveBeyond base he was murdered. Each time we remember John Kely Garçon, we praise God.

May God raise up more warriors for each and every one of our battles here on earth. May the bones that have been crushed someday rise up and rejoice. May we all encourage one another to live beyond the sin, the suffering, and the evil that surround us every day.

What battle are you called to fight?

CHAPTER 9

REAL PROBLEMS, REAL SOLUTIONS

*To live beyond means to work on solving big
problems instead of focusing on trivial ones.*

I ENDED UP STAYING ABOUT THREE WEEKS ON MY INITIAL TRIP TO Haiti following the earthquake. And for the next three years, Laurie and I led mission teams for a week each month. Progress was slow, and sometimes it appeared to me that nothing had changed since my original trip. Rubble was swept out of the streets but remained in piles at each corner. Few buildings that had fallen were resurrected. Toussaint Louverture International Airport in Port-au-Prince, Haiti's busiest airport, remained in shambles. The control tower damaged by the quake was repaired in makeshift fashion so that the many relief aid flights could land and have more direct access to those in need without having to drive over from the Dominican Republic.

In the weeks and months following the earthquake, recovering the dead, creating effective sanitation solutions, tending the injured, and feeding them and other survivors remained priorities. Thousands of relief aid workers from around the world poured into the ravaged island nation, including those from the Red Cross and Doctors Without Borders, but we saw little organized, consistent collaboration.

Every individual and agency was willing, of course, but the lack of emergency services and clear governmental leadership resulted in ongoing chaos. In fact, the lack of a clear chain of command left many national and local leaders with headaches that should have been avoidable. However, in a country where graft and corruption are assumed and even celebrated by some elected officials, many of the resources pouring in following the earthquake were delayed. Individual officials, or those claiming to be, insisted on receiving bribes or "transportation taxes" before allowing food, water, medical supplies, generators, and earth-moving equipment to reach the areas of greatest need.

As a result, my return trips to Haiti were in some ways even more horrific than the first. Even six months after the quake, most of the destruction appeared just as it did the day of the disaster. But the staggering number of casualties created new and equally dangerous problems. With the city morgue and hospitals overflowing and many bodies remaining trapped beneath rubble, streets in Port-au-Prince were literally crowded with death ...dead eyes, dead hearts, dead dreams.

In the hot tropical climate, the pervasive stench was inescapable and unlike anything I had ever experienced. Burial and disposal were complicated by conflicts between government leaders, relief workers, and voodou chieftains, who wanted to perform rituals and oversee individual burials. With tens of thousands of bodies rapidly decomposing, however, the decision to cremate bodies and dig mass graves was deemed a necessity; otherwise, decay would lead to disease and the very real possibility of a cholera epidemic.

As a doctor, I had experienced many graphic scenes and horrific events before, but none as overwhelming and surreal as what I experienced in Haiti. Some reporters compared it to the aftermath of the Holocaust, with the scorched scent of human remains constantly in the air. Others described it as a major battlefield after a war or as a three-dimensional glimpse of hell on earth. Problems like such as looting, vigilante justice, lack of law enforcement, and the language barrier only compounded our already challenging tasks.

We worked in clinics scattered throughout Port-au-Prince, but I felt like I was on another planet, one where every two steps forward resulted in five steps back. Most days there was little time to think about what to do next. We simply did whatever had to be done. I amputated more limbs than I ever imagined seeing in my entire career. Fatigue was countered by adrenaline and by the desire to do anything and everything to save the next life, feed the next child, help the next survivor.

Prayer became a constant ongoing process throughout the long, unbearably hot days. I have no doubt that my stamina didn't come from power bars and Gatorade as much as from divine empowerment.

———

In the face of such unprecedented human need, I gained a new appreciation for having the right perspective on life's problems. Suddenly, so many of the things that I—and most people— worried about back home in the States seemed trivial: whether to buy a new car or drive the old one, whether to go to this church or that one, and whether to repaint the house or wait another year.

These are not problems. Or if they are, they're "First World problems." When your home has been leveled, most of your family has been killed, and you don't know where your next meal will come from, now that's a problem. I don't mean to trivialize or dismiss the very real problems we have in the United States and other First World nations. However, even America's poverty-level citizens would be considered rich by many people in the world, certainly by most of the Haitians I know.

I discovered being part of the solution to someone else's real problem is much more satisfying than focusing on my First World problems. One experience, in particular, comes to mind, a situation in which our medical team and I were able to help four young survivors.

About three months after the January earthquake, our team ventured out to a clinic near the epicenter of the earthquake. While looting and pockets of violence continued to be an issue, a strong multinational military presence had restored safety, at least during the daylight hours. The darkness brought real danger.

We were in one such neighborhood on a particular afternoon, working out of a half-destroyed three-story building. We had seen many patients, followed up on a few previous ones, and provided food staples to hundreds of others. However, as the sun sank along the bay and a smoky darkness began to descend, we knew we needed to leave and head back to our home base. I was already beginning to feel uneasy because we were leaving long after we should have. Not only was violence a real issue but driving through a concrete wasteland in the dark with only a couple of bouncing headlights presented its own dangers. I anxiously spurred our medical team to move from triage to transit. We packed up our flatbed truck to leave the area.

That's when I saw them.

I stopped abruptly at the sight before me. Three girls were standing at our already-closed gate with their hands upturned and thrust through the bars. Their dark eyes pleaded in ways that transcended language, and several of us immediately moved to let them in. After we had shared our power bars and mixed rehydration powder into some water bottles, these three famished little ones began to revive. With the help of a translator, we learned they were sisters ranging in age from fourteen to two.

"Ki kote ou rete?" *Where do you live?* I asked.

They pointed to the sidewalk of the mean streets, the ones we were frantically trying to escape before dark.

"Ki kote manman y papa ou yo ye?" *Where are your parents?*

Visible emotion told me their answer before the oldest one pointed to the rubble nearby.

"Eske ou gen lòt fanmi?" *Do you have other family?* I continued trying to find out as much necessary information as we could without sounding like an interrogator. The two-year-old had allowed Carol, one of the women on our team, to pick her up and hold her. Carol's eyes filled with tears as she held the toddler and realized how little she weighed.

"Are you expecting a baby?" I asked the oldest sister. Her slightly rounded belly made me suspect as much.

Through tears, she described the violation she had endured. She went on to tell us how she and her sisters had stayed near the rubble where their mother and father were buried, unsure what to do or where to go. After she was raped, they learned to hide at night and had watched us attend to other patients before deciding to risk asking for our help.

At that moment, my heart broke for these girls, filled with a terrible sadness for all they had lost and had to endure, filled with rage at the predators who would prey on such defenseless innocence. These brave young sisters had been on their own for over three months.

Alone.

Starving.

Vulnerable.

Violated.

Afraid.

Hopeless.

Sometimes solutions come with proximity. It didn't take long to figure out what to do. I reached for my satellite phone, made a quick call to a well-connected friend, and soon we had a plan and a destination. The drive would take a while, but no one minded taking the long way home.

A few hours later, the sisters were fed, bathed, clothed, and protected behind twelve-foot-high walls topped by concertina wire. Settled into a Christian orphanage in a safer part of Port-au-Prince where they would be loved and cared for, the girls still had much to grieve and to process. But they had one another. And now they had a safe place where their basic needs would be met. A place where they would be loved, where the specter of their nightmare would fade away.

A place with hope.

Whenever I remember these girls, a passage of Scripture comes to mind: "For we are His workmanship, created in Christ Jesus for good works, which God prepared beforehand, that we should walk in them" (Ephesians 2:10).

Helping these four girls was a work that God had created for *me* to do. These girls had *my name* written on them . . . or maybe *their names* were written on me. Either way, these girls were waiting for me to come along, waiting for God to care for them through me.

What did I have to do to help them? I had to know how to use a telephone.

More importantly, I had to be there. Because what would have happened if I wasn't?

More than ever before, I understood why Jesus said, "Go! Go into all the world." If I hadn't gone, I couldn't have fulfilled the work that God had carefully planned for me. Work that tackled real problems, that showed real results, that affected real people.

What could be more satisfying than that?

All around you are real problems waiting to be solved. Children in failing schools, waiting to be mentored. Hungry people, waiting to be fed. Lost people, waiting to be saved.

Next time you find yourself complaining about trivialities, ask yourself, "What *real* problem can I tackle instead?" And if your life is lacking in *real* problems, go out and find some.

Then try to solve them.

That's living beyond yourself.

CHAPTER 10

AT JUST THE RIGHT TIME

To live beyond means to watch for God's timing
at work in every minute of your lives.

THERE WAS ANOTHER TIME IN THE MONTHS FOLLOWING THE earthquake when our LiveBeyond medical team all felt the immeasurable pleasure of working alongside God in the special works He'd planned for us to do. While we were typically working in various clinics in Port-au-Prince, we got a special request to work in a clinic in the village of Cabaret.

After finding Cabaret on a map, we loaded our medical team onto the back of a flatbed truck for what we assumed would be an hour and a half drive. We had one Haitian woman with us named Guerline who squeezed herself into the middle of the front seat and proceeded to give us directions. But when we made it to Cabaret, she insisted that we turn north away from the sea and into the mountains. We drove up and down over hills and into steep valleys.

When we had been on the road for about two hours, I could tell that our driver was clearly confused; however, we felt compelled to continue in this direction. Guerline clearly knew where she was taking us, so we decided to follow her guidance. The mountains became steeper, the road more winding, and the valleys deeper. Rounding a sharp curve, we saw a little lady standing in the middle of the dirt road. Upon seeing us, she started jumping up and down, signaling for us to stop. We pulled over and looked up the hillside at a small metal church building. The little lady greeted each of us with a kiss and excitedly shouted, "Mèsi Bondye! Yo isit la! Men yo blan! Mèsi Jezi! Yo isit la! Men yo blan!"

Not understanding exactly what she meant, we nicknamed her "the bird lady" because she jumped and chattered with such excitement, like an enthusiastic sparrow, kissing all of us time and again. Unloading our medical equipment, we headed up the hillside and set up a makeshift clinic in a grove of trees beside a tiny church building.

And they started coming. Seemingly from nowhere, mothers with sick babies began lining up. Fevers as high as 105 degrees Fahrenheit were ravaging the children. An infection was spreading quickly through this little village. Our well-stocked pharmacy boxes of antibiotics held the life-saving drugs needed at this very moment.

How had it worked out that we happened to get to this village at just the right time? An English-speaking Haitian finally revealed the story to us. What the "bird lady" had been trying to tell us was that she had spent the night before in fervent prayer. The children of her village were dying, and she knew they needed help. As she prayed, God told her He was sending doctors and nurses to take care of her people. She had the faith to stand in the middle of the road all morning waiting for us to arrive; she just didn't expect so many of us to be white! So as she greeted us, she was saying, "Thank you, God! They are here! But they're white! Thank you, Jesus! They are here! But they're white!"

Our team was overwhelmed that *we* were the ones God chose to answer this godly woman's prayer.

As we piled back into the truck at the end of a very long mobile medical clinic, our hearts thrilled to be connected with the Spirit of God. The long ride home in the pouring rain couldn't begin to quench our joy—the special joy that comes from doing the works that our All-Knowing Father had created just for us.

What if we had missed that day? What if we'd decided that we needed a break more than we needed to serve? What if we hadn't listened to our Haitian navigator who'd insisted that we turn away from Cabaret and head into the mountains?

We would have missed one of the greatest blessings a person can know …working alongside the Father in the works that He has planned for us. I wonder how long ago He made those plans for us.

Sometimes I like to dream of how many people He has handpicked for others to touch with His power and His love. I like to imagine His pleasure when He sees His people working well. In His famous Sermon on the Mount, Jesus tells us, "You are the light of the world. A city set on a hill cannot be hidden. Nor do people light a lamp and put it under a basket, but on a stand, and it gives light to all in the house. In the same way, let your light shine before others, so that they *may see your good works* and give glory to your Father who is in Heaven" (Matthew 5:14–16, emphasis mine). Others can see Jesus in us through our good works. But we have to be there to do them.

My wife likes to say, "Working in Haiti is constantly irritating but instantly gratifying." Working in Haiti is difficult. It's hot. People are desperate, and sometimes that means they don't act very nicely. But it is a delight to work alongside God in His timeless design. Our lives make a difference when we work with the Lord.

We saw this especially during the cholera epidemic that followed the earthquake. A missionary friend of ours was desperate for some help in a cholera clinic in Cap-Haïtien, so David, who had recently graduated from college and moved to Haiti full-time to organize clinics for MMDR, John Mark, and I made our way up there to help in his clinic. David had taken some supplies to this clinic in December 2010 and worked for a week, relieving a Haitian doctor who was nearly dead on his feet from exhaustion. My trip with the boys was in January 2011, and the circumstances had not improved much.

Cholera, as described by the World Health Organization, is an "acute diarrheal disease that can kill within hours if left untreated." Most cases are mild, but patients with severe cases can die within hours from dehydration. Oral rehydration solutions are a very important part of treatment, but if a patient is too weak to drink, intravenous therapy is critical. If a patient can make it beyond the first day, they stand a chance for survival. But that one day of misery takes a terrible toll on the human body.

David, John Mark, and I were ankle-deep in vomit and diarrhea as we tended to patients. Unfortunately, we were also responsible for removing the bodies of those who did not survive from the clinic. The work in a cholera clinic is taxing but doesn't require much medical training, so while the boys checked IVs and mopped the floors interminably, I made regular rounds with patients and then attempted to use some clout as a medical doctor to call in more volunteers and supplies. The skeleton crew with whom we worked and tried to relieve was hanging on by a thread.

Just when it felt like things couldn't get much worse, we ran out of IV bags. The clinic had run out many times before, a common occurrence in an emergency situation like that. The boys and I had brought water, IVs, and supplies with us, but one can only carry so much on a flight and our patients needed more. We gathered with all the other volunteers and started praying that God would provide. And, miraculously, He did. A short while later, a Doctors Without Borders truck showed up *just* to give us a supply of IVs, and then left. One of my calls made it to the right person, and the Lord blessed our work. Some of those patients still died. But those who lived and died saw the love of Jesus through the volunteers and my family as we cared for their needs. God allowed His light to shine through us, and then He blessed us, just when we needed Him the most.

———

When we teamed up with the Mormon group after the earth-quake, they lent us a flatbed truck that we drove into Port-au-Prince twice a day to transport injured patients to the hospital. One afternoon, I was on such a drive because the orthopedic staff at our makeshift hospital was working at full throttle and my surgical services were not needed at the time. Our team had a system: we drove the flatbed through town with the windows down, listening for people screaming or crying for help. We would push through to them, start an IV and stabilize their conditions, and get them on the flatbed. When we had twenty-five to thirty patients, it was time to head back to the hospital. The drive was terribly uncomfortable for our poor patients as the roads were cracked, riddled with potholes, and filled with rubble.

On this particular day, we heard a man yelling for help. We saw that he was caught by the legs under a slab of concrete. The side of a building had collapsed in the days since the earthquake and had fallen on this man. Our team was unable to move the giant hunk of concrete, but a group of Haitians working in the rubble nearby came over to help. Together we got the man out of the building, stabilized, and into the truck. I turned to thank the men who had helped us. My Haitian Creole at the time was quite primitive (arguably, it still is) so I just thanked everyone in English. To my surprise, one man replied with, "No problem!" in a thick Boston accent. We immediately got to talking.

Bobby was born in Haiti, but his parents moved to the United States when he was young. He grew up in Boston and Philadelphia. A few years before the earthquake, he came back to marry his beloved wife and find a way to help in his country. He and his wife had started an orphanage and hospice in Thomazeau, Haiti. When the earthquake struck, he went from having 10 kids to close to 40, overnight. He had some very sick children, so he asked us to go see them. I agreed, and we went to see him in Thomazeau later that day. Their conditions were worse than we'd thought. A few of the children died the night we arrived. Distraught, I made a pact with myself that I would visit these children every month when we came to Haiti.

As soon as my son David graduated from college in May 2010, he moved to Haiti to help facilitate clinics. He volunteered to work with a couple in Port-au-Prince. They left as soon as he got there for a brief reprieve and put him in charge of their house and clinic facility—a pretty big task for a twenty-two-year-old. But he was up to it. He ran the operations and supplies for the clinic and managed the medical teams we sent down throughout the summer. When things quieted down in Port-au-Prince, David moved to Bobby's orphanage.

David has always had a way with hitting it off with people from the start. His charismatic smile, bright blue eyes, and extroverted personality have a way of bringing down people's defenses. He wasted no time getting to know everyone he could in Thomazeau. Bobby introduced him to his friends, and their friendship deepened. Thomazeau became more than just a stop on our journey—it was often our destination.

It was around this time that Laurie and I began our contemplation and prayer regarding moving to Haiti full-time. The country of Haiti was transitioning from disaster mode to survival mode, and while MMDR technically started as a disaster relief organization, we were thinking about what we could do to convert our efforts into development. We felt as if traveling to Haiti every month was good work, but it wasn't having a lasting impact. We wanted to achieve better results, and we felt that the Lord was calling us there permanently. So we contemplated owning land. We planned to make a point of supporting the orphanage, but we still didn't feel tied specifically to Thomazeau.

David was our scout for looking for land for us to purchase to use as a base in Haiti. He traveled all over the country in search of land we could afford. Undeveloped land in Haiti is expensive—more expensive than most people realize. It was my dream to build a hospital. Haiti's hospital services are understaffed and underfunded, so this was a chance to bring higher standards into an area in great need. Laurie and I also dreamed of a guesthouse so that American teams could regularly visit to serve in different capacities. Most of the parcels of land that we looked at would not accommodate this dream.

After a frustrating trip to northern Haiti, David went out for an afternoon walk. He hadn't seen his farmer friends in a while, so he decided to visit them. But then something pushed him farther down the road. And that's when he found it: 63 acres of land ready to be sold. It was owned by a Voodou priest who had rented out parcels of land to local subsistence farmers. He had recently decided that it was time to get out of that business and sell the land for good. The price was good, much better than we would find anywhere else. And after walking it,

David realized that it got a pretty consistent breeze off of Lake Azuéi, a large inland lake near Thomazeau. He called Bobby, and Bobby confirmed that the land was for sale. Then David called me, and we started drawing up plans.

On January 10, 2012, that parcel of land became the site for LiveBeyond's base. We love to think that it was transferred from the kingdom of darkness to the Kingdom of Light. It would be over a year before Laurie and I actually moved to Haiti, but purchasing the land was our first big step. God led us to that land in His timing. Now it was time for Laurie and me to surrender to His plan and go outside our comfort zone to learn to defend the cause of the oppressed.

CHAPTER 11

HOW TO KNOW GOD

To live beyond means to defend the cause
of the poor and the oppressed.

SHEER TERROR GRIPPED THE BOY STANDING BEFORE ME.

He looked about four years old, but his mouth full of teeth suggested he was more likely eight. His head was bowed in chronic despair, his dull eyes cast down directly in front of his calloused, dusty feet. He wore what might have once been a man's polo shirt, now filthy brown and thin with wear, turned inside out and backward.

He stood as still as a statue, while pus streamed down both brown cheeks. He had pink eye. He reeked of stale sweat and the sickening stench of infection. His knees trembled, and his pulse beat wildly in his tiny neck—I could tell he was paralyzed by unimaginable fear.

At that moment, I said a prayer and hoped we could help him.

That he would let us help him.

That others would let us help him.

———

Our day had started there in Ghana with a brilliant sunrise piercing the African horizon like a fiery sword. I was there with a few other LiveBeyond team members, including our oldest son, David, treating as many native villagers in need as possible. While Laurie and I had already made our decision to move to Haiti and the wheels were in motion, LiveBeyond continued to go wherever a need created an opportunity to expand the Kingdom.

Established as an independent republic in 1957 when the Gold Coast region of Africa proclaimed independence from the United Kingdom, Ghana is one of the more developed countries on a continent often defined by its struggles. While modern health care exists in most urban areas surrounding modern cities such as Kumasi and the Ghanaian capital of Accra, outlying regions and villages often lack medicine, vaccines, and adequate care. In these rural areas, disease, malnutrition, and poor hygiene often go unattended.

The Republic of Ghana has numerous natural resources along with a strategic location on the Atlantic Ocean and the Gulf of Guinea. These two positives, however, have also created some new and unique challenges. Drug runners often use Ghanaian ports to transfer illegal shipments from South America to dealers in Europe and Asia. Human trafficking has increased as well, and not just in the sex trade. More and more children in developing African countries like Ghana are being sold into forced labor as well as prostitution.

So the need in Ghana is great—both medically and spiritually.

The jarring call to morning prayer from the local mosque faded with the dawn and was quickly replaced by the clanking of the bustling African village that was our temporary base. As our boat parted the calm waters of Lake Volta and pointed toward the day's destination, the island of Bakpa, our remote area medical team contemplated our mission. Ostensibly, we were in this remote region of Ghana to provide health care to the local tribes. In reality, we were there working alongside Touch A Life, the organization founded by Pam Cope. Our first mission was for the purpose of performing surgery on former child slaves. Our subsequent missions were to continue with medical care and clean water projects.

West Africa has a long and acrimonious relationship with slavery. Slave masters have plied their nefarious trade here from antiquity, and the profession hasn't diminished with the advent of technology. It seems unbelievable that human beings can be bought and sold in the twenty-first century, but it happens every day. Often sold by their own people, West African slaves have wound up in every corner of the world.

Well-known countries such as France, England, and the United States have shared the ignominy of slavery with less well-known of Haiti, Egypt, and Algiers. While the underpinnings of the trade always seem to center on money, I'm convinced the evil extends far beyond. Those individuals disenfranchised due to age, gender, or conquest become profit for the powerful and marks for the sadistic. Formerly, the slaves were exported to other countries, but our pursuit that day was local.

The motives remain largely economic. Ghanaian parents, who rarely use birth control, might have ten children and become overwhelmed by the need to support their family. Eventually it becomes apparent they can sell six to feed the remaining four. In this region, many children under the age of five will be sold into slavery by their own families.

In today's market, children around the age of four are typically sold for about twenty USD. The girls will become house slaves or enter the sex trade; the boys are consigned to a life of forced labor in the fishing industry. They are beaten, starved, and made to work excruciating hours until they either die or decide they can outrun their masters. Their childhood, which rightfully should be filled with love, security, and education, is replaced by hate, fear, and danger. Surrounded by friends who lived free with their parents, they remained slaves in their own country, their only crime being one of the many sold into slavery.

These innocents were our quarry.

———

Our little boat ground to a halt against the muddy beach as inquisitive children quickly enveloped us. Unaccustomed to Western faces, they were fascinated with our pale skin, light hair, and sunglasses. As news spread of our arrival, stone-faced elders quickly replaced the children as our welcoming committee. Since few visitors came to the island, let alone those from America, the arrival of white faces caused concern. For centuries, such arrivals by outsiders usually brought calamity.

Using our interpreter and visual aids from our medical bags, we indicated our purpose. When the islanders were convinced that we'd come in peace, my son David and I were ushered to the chief's hut. "*Akwaaba!*" we heard, a native greeting meaning "welcome." Chief Parka was a diminutive, bright-eyed, smiling man with an understated royal bearing, the undisputed leader of his people. He asked me in English to explain our reason for visiting his island.

In tribal Ghana, if you fell into the good graces of the village chief, he would allow you to work under a mango tree where the equatorial sun was relieved by partial shade. If he wasn't impressed or didn't trust you, he would relegate you to an unshaded, parched plot where the unrelenting heat would wilt you like a desert flower. Since our mission of health care and clean water pleased him, we got the mango tree.

But our negotiation wasn't complete—we wanted to rescue child slaves. So in return for our offered assistance, we asked him to use his influence as chief to help us locate and release enslaved children from their masters. I wasn't particularly optimistic, but sometimes a direct, open-handed approach works best. Plus, I knew our mission would be more successful if we had the chief on our side. Surprisingly, the lure of free health care and clean water for his people overcame any reluctance he may have felt to confront the slave masters.

We unloaded our medical supplies and quickly began setting up our mobile medical clinic. The sight of unfamiliar American faces laboring under the sprawling branches of the mango tree drew more villagers, some out of curiosity and others because they heard about the life-saving medicine we brought with us.

The unbroken stream of the sick, disabled, and curious continued long into the afternoon. As our medical team dove into the overwhelming tide of the sick and our prayer team offered the Gospel, someone shoved a little boy into our midst.

A little boy who had been taught to be terrified of us.

In a cruel attempt to fully control their minions, local slave masters tell the children never to go with Americans. They tell the children that foreigners will torture, kill, and eat them. The irony, of course, was not lost on us since these thugs not only buy and sell children but treat them worse than any dog is allowed to be treated in the States. So at that moment, fully convinced of his impending demise, this dear child was doing his best to remain stoic and brave.

One of our translators leaned in and quickly confirmed that this boy was indeed a slave. Our spokesman then communicated to this child that we were there to help him, to free him, and to take him to a safe place where he would be cared for. Still tentative and uncertain of what was about to happen, the boy's fear began to melt as our medical veterans gently began to examine him and proceed with necessary treatments.

Soon he had been cleaned, dressed, fed, and medicated, and was lovingly held in the arms of a dear woman on our team.

As the afternoon began to wind down, our translator found me and discreetly pointed out a young man leaning against a wall several yards away. Tall and muscular, he stood with arms crossed and eyes boring holes through us, clearly ready for a fight. No translation was needed for me to know what this tough guy wanted. He had come to reclaim his "property."

I grabbed my son David—you may remember, he's about 6' 4" and 250 pounds of muscle—and the two of us showed no trepidation approaching our would-be nemesis. The translator came along, and in no uncertain terms we made it clear to this master that he had lost a slave. Although he argued, I could tell the slave owner was much more afraid of us than we of him. I'd be afraid, too, with a foreign stranger as big as my son looking down at me. David has that rare ability to smile as though he's having the time of his life, knowing he's scaring someone to death.

But violence wasn't necessary. When Chief Parka approached and gruffly spoke to the young man, this fight was clearly over before it started. We refused to simply buy the boy; that would mean that he had money in his pocket to purchase another child as soon as we left. Unhappy at the prospect of losing his investment but cowed by our determination, the defeated man scowled and turned to jog down the dirt trail away from the village.

The jubilation we felt rivaled that of Rocky after the big match. Good defeated evil that afternoon, and one little boy's life would never be the same.

Heading back to our base camp, we were exhausted but also grateful. We watched the sun setting in a burst of crimson glory, its rays reflecting off the dull gray lake like sparkling rubies. As we aimed our bow toward the mainland, our little boat felt lighter and freer with our newest addition, little Kwame, on board. Even though his countenance suggested that he didn't trust us, his heart knew otherwise. His belly was full, and he was clean and clothed for the first time in years.

He was free.

With no living family that he knew of, Kwame adapted quickly for someone who had been enslaved for at least half his life. We took him to the Christian orphanage run by PACODEP, a Ghanaian organization that works tirelessly to rescue children from slavery, where he found a home that was bright and clean and full of new friends. He quickly became the new champion of the soccer field, enjoyed the unimaginable number of three meals a day, went to school, and most of all simply felt safe. Little did he know that two of the women who were with us on this mission were soon to become his mother and grandmother, for he was officially adopted within a few years of his rescue.

We returned to Kete Krachi, Ghana, several times over the years working with the fine PACODEP team to spread the Good News of Jesus by providing medical care and clean water to various tribes in the region. By God's grace, our team was able to help liberate five other children from the toxic grip of slavery.

———

For most of my life, I have had a desire to know the Lord. From childhood, my parents told me about Jesus, teaching me and leading me to follow Him. Since being baptized when I was eleven years old, I have spent my entire life wanting a close relationship with God.

I've prioritized having a morning Bible study. Daily, I try to enter into His presence with worship. I enjoy reading books that teach me more about His nature. So it came as quite a shock to me when I happened across this Scripture: "He defended the cause of the poor and needy, and so all went well. Isn't this what it means *to know Me*?" declares the Lord. (Jeremiah 22:16, emphasis mine.)

In reading this passage, I actually did a double take. *Did that just say what I think it said? Did God just tell me how I can get to know Him? Why haven't I heard this message before?* After all my reading, listening, and studying, why didn't I know that God had made it clear about the way we can get to know Him?

I read this passage over and over again. I meditated on it. I ask God Himself about it. And I finally realized that it means just what it says. It's really quite clear. Do you hear the simplicity in this passage? God Himself tells us how we can get to know Him. He says to *defend the cause of the poor and the needy*. That's what it means to know God.

I fear this phenomenally huge piece of our relationship with the Creator has been ignored by a large part of the church and vilified as "social activism" by even more. Unfortunately, the biblical mandate of taking care of the poor has been sacrificed on the altar of political correctness. More often than not, the Western churchgoing culture thinks that being a Christian simply means avoiding the "big sins" and making sure you go to church every week. No wonder so many of us don't know God.

Defending the cause of the poor and needy . . . how in the world do you do that? What does it mean? Surely, this is a

daunting task. The causes of the poor and the needy are complicated, messy, and vast. Defending their causes implies risk.

When I think of defending something, I think of football. My father-in-law, Gene Stallings, is called "Coach" by
my three brothers-in-law and myself. As a young boy dating
Coach's daughter, even more than I enjoyed going to the Dallas
Cowboy games, I loved riding home from Texas Stadium in
the car with Coach, listening to his review of the game. He
would talk through the game-changing plays, giving insights
that most fans never hear. I was smart enough to keep my
mouth shut and just listen as he would tell how a cornerback would key off a receiver watching to see whether he
stepped off with his right or left foot. The safety would time
his blitz when a particular quarterback jerked his head in a
certain direction during the snap count. Coach would describe
that if the tight end shuffled prior to the snap it meant that
the defensive back could anticipate the play in order to be in
the right place at the right time to prevent the offense from
completing a pass. I learned from Coach that strong men use
their God-given talents to defend their territory. I learned that
to be a good defender, you had to anticipate the plans of the
offense. I learned that defense wins games.

So how does this relate to knowing God? Why in the
world does defending the cause of the poor and the needy
allow us to know God?

———

I like to work with wood. My grandfather, whom I never really
knew, passed down an old motorized lathe for turning and
carving wood. Sometimes I think I enjoyed working with the

lathe just to feel close to my granddad. I fixed up a wood-working shop in the barn at our farm and I would go down there at night to turn table legs and pedestals, enjoying the aroma of the freshly turned wood. My daughter, Jacklyn, would come and watch. She started with candlesticks. After watching me and using my leftovers, Jacklyn would take her turn with the lathe, turning out simple items that she would take upstairs to show her brothers.

Did Jacklyn want a new hobby? No. Did she want to create something beautiful? No. She wanted to be with her daddy. Our time in the barn was just that—*our* time. We were working together. She watched me, imitated me, and did the work I was doing. As we worked together, we talked. Well, actually, she did most of the talking and I listened. She told me about her triumphs and her disappointments. She spelled out her dreams and formulated her goals. I knew all about her friends, her grades, her favorite teachers, her plans, and her loves. She drank in every word I said to her. She eagerly sought my advice, wanting to please me, wanting to know if I approved of who she was and who she was becoming. In these hours, I was able to pass on to her my love and admiration. I was able to give her my blessing. My beautiful, gifted daughter and I got to know each other very well.

It's the same for us with God. How do we get to know Him? We work with Him. We go into His workshop. We watch Him. We imitate Him. And we get His blessing. We get to know Him by doing His work.

Our problem is that we too often think God's work is all about us. We think that His focus is on giving us more satisfying lives. We expect Him to work for us to bring us fulfillment. But the truth is, God is at work for the cause of the poor. God's names are: "Father of the fatherless," "Protector of widows," "Hope of the hopeless." He is the "Defender of the poor." If we want to know God, we work beside Him . . . defending the cause of the poor and needy. Which brings me back to football.

Defense implies offense. There's no reason to have a defender if there's not an offender. Defense also implies an object that needs defending. On the football field, it's the goal line. In the world, it's the poor. I've listened for hours, watched film, pored over playbooks, and come to a minimal under-standing of football strategy. I just don't have the mind for it. But what's the strategy for defending the poor? Who is the offender? How can I relate the job of a safety or cornerback to my work with the poor?

I've watched defensive football players sacrifice their bodies time and again to bring down a running back or receiver. Aches and sprains are part of the game. My wife remembers a Cowboys game when Charlie Waters and Cliff Harris were so poured out with exhaustion that they didn't even know the final score. Fans expect to see players exhausting themselves on the field for the sake of the game.

Can that apply to us as we defend the poor? Can we stra-tegically set up ourselves with a plan to outsmart the offender, to anticipate his game plan, to defend our territory, and to win the game? Are we expected to exhaust ourselves and pour ourselves out for the cause of the poor? God gives us the answer in Isaiah 58:10, "If you pour yourself out for the hungry and satisfy the desire of the afflicted, then shall your light rise in the darkness and your gloom be as the noonday."

We *are* expected to exhaust ourselves on this playing field. We *are* expected to be defenders. We are expected to formulate a game-winning strategy. Our playing field is the world of the lost; our objects to defend are the poor; the offender is Satan, and our game plan is to transfer the oppressed from the kingdom of darkness into the Kingdom of light.

As a defender, we must understand that there is someone on the offensive who will not appreciate our new role as a defender. We may get hurt, insulted, slandered, and defamed. We might be misunderstood or ignored by people who once claimed to care about us. We will get our hands dirty and be forced to move out of our comfort zone. The people we are serving, assisting, and protecting might be radically different from us. And they may not even appreciate our efforts. We have to decide if we're ready to defend someone who doesn't share our values, language, or skin color. Even our religion, education level, or political party. We have to decide if we're willing to risk injury or death for them.

Jesus did.

In fact, He was willing to die in order to save them. He wasn't just willing to die. He died willingly, and not just for the people who knew they needed help. He died for the very people who betrayed and killed Him. He died for people like you and me. "But God shows His love for us in that while we were still sinners, Christ died for us" (Romans 5:7).

His sacrifice was definitely not something we deserved. But He loves us so much that He did what we could not do for ourselves—He died so we could live. He defended us from the accuser and rescued us from ourselves. He did not shrink back from the aches and pains and strains of being a defender. He poured Himself out and left everything on the playing field. He blitzed across the scrimmage line and tackled the offensive one.

He knew His territory and He marched into hell to defend His own. And we all know who was victorious in that contest!

If we want to know God, we'll live just like that.

———

Rescuing Kwame and five other boys from slavery in Ghana gave me a thrill unlike any I had ever experienced. By the end of that mission, I felt like I'd played in and won the Super Bowl. Watching six former child slaves play soccer felt like receiving the trophy for Associated Press NFL Defensive Player of the Year. I had defended the cause of these children, and I felt the glow of Heaven. I had discovered a secret that Scripture had whispered ... "Take care of the poor and you will get to know me; sacrifice your own life and you'll find real life; live beyond yourself and my light will shine on you."

CHAPTER 12

CALLED TO HAITI

To live beyond means going outside your comfort zone.

THE DECISION TO UPROOT OURSELVES FROM OUR HOME IN Tennessee and relocate permanently to Haiti wasn't made overnight. Laurie and I had talked and dreamed about such a radical lifestyle change for some time. Even when we were dating in high school and college, we believed we should "dream big." Yes, we were young and idealistic, naïve to some of the realities of life, and not as mature in our faith. But the funny thing is, our dream of serving together in some radical way never disappeared.

After the earthquake in Haiti and our subsequent trips to provide aid there, my wife and I continued to see both our futures tethered to this work. During the three years between the earthquake and our move, we served in other places— Africa, the Middle East, Central America—also impoverished and desperately in need. But something about the people of Haiti had captured both our hearts.

Laurie first went to Haiti in March 2010, about two months after the earthquake. When she saw the devastation in Haiti, unlike what we had seen anywhere else in the world, she became acutely aware of the fact that these were the United States' neighbors, *our* neighbors, and it was our job to care for them. She also saw that there was a veil of Christianity in Haiti but that the country operated under Voodou. She felt the need of evangelism heavy on her heart.

But Laurie knew something was special about Haiti even before the earthquake took us there. In late 2009, months before the earthquake hit in January 2010, Laurie was praying to the Lord about where MMDR should serve next. Our work on the clinic we built in Honduras was finishing up, and we didn't feel that Honduras was exactly where the Lord wanted us in the long-term. During her prayers, she felt that the Lord told her that we were supposed to work in Haiti. Neither of us had ever been to Haiti or even knew anyone who had been to Haiti. She felt that it was out of the blue, so she told me about it and continued to contemplate the idea until I left for disaster relief following the earthquake. Then she knew the confirmation of what the Lord told her.

The things that she witnessed on her first trip to Haiti affirmed in her that the Lord guided our steps to this country for a reason. She jumped headfirst into the work. She did all the prep for the teams in terms of coordinating flights, loading supplies, and keeping teams organized when we made it to Haiti. For several months, a large bank in Alabama generously donated the use of their corporate jets to send medical personnel and supplies to Haiti. Laurie would load up the trucks and drive them to Birmingham to fill the flights. Laurie and I worked and dreamed and prayed together about a future in Haiti.

Many nights we got down on our knees to pray. We asked God about *His* plans for our future. We wanted to know what *He* wanted us to do with all His blessings. We wanted to know how we might answer *His* call. We wanted to know if we could live in *His* lifestyle. We both knew that such a prayer was audacious, even dangerous. We were volunteering to give up control. We were volunteering to give up prestige. We were volunteering to give up our savings. We were volunteering to give up *everything*.

We were volunteering to answer His calling on our lives.

We know that Jesus is our perfect example. Our Lord gave up His riches. He put aside His power. He relinquished His glory. He left His family. He lived as a poor man. Then He died. He did this so that we may follow Him into eternal life.

While we had many supporters, a lot of people were telling us we were nuts because we had a great medical practice and a great lifestyle. Who would want to throw that away? Among them were people we admire and respect, so it wasn't easy for Laurie and me to make a decision against their advice. It was nerve-racking, especially for me, to step outside the status quo on a different path. I'm the kind of guy who wants to know exactly how things play out. So as I contemplated selling our farm, our house, our cars, dissolving my medical practice, and leaving all the things we'd spent a lifetime gathering, I couldn't help but wonder if I was making the right choice as the head of the family. Selfishly, I wondered if I would miss certain things like my guitar collection. (I can tell you now that I don't.)

But I knew that my life didn't look like Jesus's life, and that convicted me. His Spirit prompted me to want to make sweeping changes in order to become like Him. Answering His call to serve in Thomazeau, Haiti, and choosing to live beyond the status quo to join Jesus in relieving the pain of the oppressed has not been easy. It's been, by far, the hardest, most challenging, and most back-breaking job I've ever known. Yet this choice has brought me tangible joy, genuine peace, fulfilling pleasure . . . abundant life.

This radical call of Jesus is for every Christian.

This call to follow our Leader in His lifestyle is His invitation to all of His believers. His example is to leave our old lifestyle behind in order to become like Him. He didn't *exclude* anyone when He commanded His followers to "Go." He wants us to be leavers. *Believers should be leavers!* The first step of being like Jesus is to leave. Just as He left Heaven, we leave our old ways, our old habits, our old pursuits, and even our homes and families.

One of my favorite passages describing Jesus is 2 Corinthians 8:9: "For you know the grace of our Lord Jesus Christ, that though He was rich, yet for your sake, He became poor so that you by His poverty you might become rich."

Here I see how Jesus made the choice to live beyond His wealth, His power, His prestige, His position, and His family (everything that made Him rich) ... in order to allow us to live and live abundantly.

But, for most of my life, I had chosen to live comfortably. I had chosen to enjoy wealth, to appreciate prestige, to take pleasure in my position, and to relish the affection of my family. I graduated from a Christian university. I attended church three times a week. I had daily Bible studies. I loved being a reputable doctor in the United States. I loved having an income that allowed me to take our family on vacations—and to do disaster relief work—wherever we wanted. I loved having disposable wealth to spend on myself so that I could fly airplanes and purchase fancy guitars and take my family to the best restaurants and have community respect. But Jesus didn't have or want any of that. It finally dawned on me that if my Lord, the Almighty Creator of the universe, could leave His riches and live among the poor in order to bring them life, then surely I could follow Him by leaving my home in America and do the same.

———

As I pondered my ability to follow Jesus, I still had questions. *What does it mean to live out my faith on a whole new level? Do I really want to be like Jesus in these ways? Can I actually live like Jesus? Do I have enough faith to leave like Jesus?*

I realized that answering the radical call of Jesus would require a fundamental transformation of my heart. A slight tweaking wouldn't bring about the necessary adjustment. For me, His call necessitated a profound lifestyle change. I was like the rich young ruler, contemplating giving up everything to serve Him. Accepting Jesus as my role model meant more than just an attitude adjustment.

It meant I would have to die.

The bottom line was that I needed to die to myself in order to begin living like Him.

I realized that answering the radical call is not about continuing the status quo with a veneer of Christianity. It's not about continuing to live the American dream with the simple addition of a church service or Bible study each week. It is not about decorating our homes with crosses and Scriptures. And it's not about wanting more out of life—more meaning, more joy, more excitement, or more fulfillment.

The radical call is about willingly letting go of everything regarding *ourselves* and sacrificing for *others*. It's following Jesus into a lifestyle of abandoning our wants and our needs in order to serve the wants and needs of others.

It's not being *willing* to let go, but willingly letting go.

It's not being *willing* to die, but dying willingly.

━━━━

I suspect many of us—maybe most of us—are able to sit in church and say, "Yes, I'm willing to sacrifice for Jesus." But very few ever do. After years and years of talking about sacrifice, the time came to put some actions to my words.

One morning, while I was having my alone time with the Lord, Laurie walked in the room. I asked her the question I had just asked myself, "What did you do yesterday that required faith?" I had been reading the "Hall of Faith" in Hebrews 11, noticing just how many risks these incredible believers took for their faith. Just like me, she hemmed and hawed and stumbled over her answer. She admitted that she had been very busy and had done quite a few good things, but when she was honest with herself, just like me, she admitted that nothing she had done had required any faith. We were beginning to realize that risk is a component of faith. Abraham left an advanced, comfortable civilization to go live in tents in an unknown land to receive his promises from God. By faith, Moses led his people out of the security of Egypt into the salvation of the desert. Rahab, David, Samuel, and many others risked their lives for their faith. "And all these, though commended through their faith, did not receive what was promised." (Hebrews 11:39) How much more faith should we have, knowing that God's promises are fulfilled in Jesus?

From then on, we asked each other every day, "What did you do today that required faith?" Later, we began asking more difficult questions. "Did you sacrifice for anyone today, or were you just willing to sacrifice? Did you live beyond yourself?"

At first, we had difficulty answering these questions. Some days our responses were embarrassing. These simple questions illuminated the difference between what we were *willing to do* and what we were *actually doing*. After each of these conversations, we reminded each other that Jesus said, "If you cling to your life, you will lose it; but if you give up your life for me, you will find it" (Matthew 10:39 NLT).

The Lord was using these questions to require us to perform a self-audit. And our audit showed a balance sheet that was out of balance. We had to admit to ourselves that we had been clinging to our own lives. While we had the full intention of living for Jesus, we were actually living for ourselves.

The powerful conviction of the Holy Spirit convinced me of the truth. My lifestyle did not look like the lifestyle of Jesus Christ. I did not have many activities that required faith. My intentions did not match my reality. My time was spent providing for myself and the ones I loved instead of providing for the poor. It was time for me to admit who was the master of my life. Was it Almighty God or was it me? Was I going to continue living for myself, or was I going to give up my life for Him?

———

We continued to talk and pray about our decision. As we began to feel God's Spirit calling us to do something that sounded rather crazy, we shared it with our children and extended families. We felt that God might be calling us to sell what we had in order to move and work full-time in Haiti. Amazingly, they were all on board! Our kids seemed more excited than we were and committed to doing anything and everything to help. David had been living in Haiti off and on for a while as he got his master's from Texas A&M; John Mark was in the international studies department at Texas A&M and leader of the Texas A&M LiveBeyond student group, and Jacklyn was finishing up high school, all set to become an Aggie after graduation. Our parents and siblings were also supportive, even as they expressed their concerns. Our closest circle of friends and our church community only reinforced our calling.

Laurie and I continued to pose our daily question to one another over dinner, "What did you do today that required faith?" We habitually prayed and sought the presence of God and found that He was leading us in works that proved our faith. He led us in ways that required risk. We found ourselves doing things that, with God's help, we would survive, but without Him, we would fall flat on our faces. We were able to look one another in the eye and laughingly say, "You wouldn't believe what happened today! Yes, I did something that required faith." But even though the things we did in Tennessee were good things, they were nothing in comparison to the martyrs and missionaries in Haiti and around the world. And we desperately desired to follow in their footsteps.

God's call to us was to exercise our faith outside of our home, on alien soil. It was a call to work with people who needed to hear the truth of Jesus, not the people who had heard of Him every day of their lives. It was a call to Haiti.

I admit that I had some sleepless nights as we reached this decision. Many evenings I tossed and turned as my brain ran through possible scenarios.

What would we do if it didn't work out?

What if there is a Haitian revolution?

What if we can't make ends meet?

What will my colleagues think of me?

What is it going to be like to actually live in a country like Haiti?

Can I live without the amenities I have grown accustomed to in the United States?

Is God really going to take care of us?

Will we be able to pay for our children's college tuition?

He had a comforting word for my every question. When I asked if I could live without the conveniences to which I was so accustomed, He whispered, "Let me tell you a secret: Your possessions get in the way of an abundant life."

When I admitted my fear of being broke for the rest of my life, He responded, "The investments that you make now in the lives of the poor are deposits that will be your financial currency in the age to come."

When I confessed my dread of being considered unsuccessful by family and colleagues, I heard His reply, "Success is determined by knowing and understanding me." He had an answer for every doubt I could throw at Him.

Finally, sitting in our den in 2011, Laurie and I made the ultimate decision to sell our things—our home, our farm, our furniture—and use the money to serve the people of Haiti full-time. We knew it wouldn't be easy, but we also knew God's faithfulness trumped any obstacle we would surely encounter. After lots of talk and fervent prayer, we answered the call. Finally, we were fully on board to partner with the Lord in the works He had prepared for us.

Logistically, we had a lot of work to do. Talk about a new set of problems! I had a medical practice to dismantle. We had a home to sell and connections to uproot. But neither of us had any sense of peace doing anything else. We couldn't ignore the knock of the needy we heard at the door of our hearts. God never ignores us, and now we could not ignore the people in need whom He had placed in our lives.

We decided to wait to move until Jacklyn was out of high school. Little did we know that logistically we wouldn't actually move until the end of her freshman year at Texas A&M. Due to how often we were gone every month and summer to Haiti for medical clinics, we knew she deserved to live in a stable environment with us until she graduated from high school. We did some remodeling on our house before we put it on the market around Christmas 2012. It sold fairly quickly, and we made a profit on the sale. Our farm took a little longer. We put it on the market long before we sold our house, and I actually had to fly back from Haiti for the closing.

Closing the practice was difficult both personally and logistically. It was emotionally taxing to send patients I had spent years getting to know to other offices. And selling the equipment piece by piece was no walk in the park. But the money we made went into our work in Haiti.

There is no more humbling experience than selling, giving, and throwing away the things you spent a lifetime accumulating. At our spring fundraiser in Nashville, we put all the higher end items that we'd collected over the years (crystal, china, and so on—things we wouldn't need in Haiti) into a silent auction. A lot of that stuff was given to us as wedding presents and had seen us through our entire marriage. I still remember watching a woman walk out of the fundraiser with one of our favorite bowls. It was from Florence, Italy, and we always used it for bowtie pasta meals. As I watched that bowl slip out the door, I thought, *That's our memories going out of the door, never to come back.* It was little moments like that that made the whole thing feel real.

What we couldn't sell in the silent auction or a garage sale, we gave away. And everything we couldn't give away we had to throw away. Imagine our surprise when some of our most treasured possessions ended up in a landfill!

On May 14, 2013, Laurie and I officially moved to Haiti. On all of our other trips to Haiti, we had teams of about 40 people with us, at least 80 bags, and the strenuous task of trying to keep up with all of them. It was a big production. But on the day we left, there was no production, no sending-off party, no excitement—just the two of us holding hands with one hand and clutching most of our worldly possessions in the other. It was lonely, quiet, and solemn, as if our lives were about to change forever.

Because our guesthouse was still under construction, we spent our first night at the guesthouse of a nonprofit located about 5 miles from our base called Hope for Haiti's Children. A week later, they had a big team coming in, so we relocated to the concrete slab on which our guesthouse was being built. It was the beginning of the hurricane season. We slept on military cots, we had no running water, no security, no privacy, no electricity other than the solar panel batteries that charged our phones, and an outhouse near our equipment storage garage. I remember waking up with a goat in my face one morning, and let's face it, that early in the morning, their eyes look quite demonic. Looking back, I realize how naive we were, but I think God was kind because we were fully relying on Him. At this point, I was still reveling in the fact that we actually did it, we actually moved. God knew that to prepare for the lessons He would teach us in Haiti, Laurie and I needed to be outside of our comfort zone.

CHAPTER 13

THE ECONOMY OF THE KINGDOM

To live beyond means to give generously,
investing in the Kingdom economy.

LAURIE AND I ENJOY PLAYING A FUN LITTLE GAME THAT'S BECOME
an unofficial tradition on our wedding anniversaries. Each year,
over dinner, we think back and recite the various places in
which we've celebrated our anniversaries through all the prior
years. I can't remember exactly when we started this tradition,
but we quickly realized each year's particular place or restau-
rant reflects the various stages of our lives and marriage at the
time. I'm sure this is true of most couples.

While it was never fast food during those early years when
I was in medical school and residency, the restaurants we chose
accurately reflected our financial status. As I finished my surgery
training and our financial standing improved, the restaurants
and venues became more exclusive, exotic, and expensive. We
celebrated in London, Florence, and Jerusalem. Our travels
were exciting, and the meals were delicious, but honestly, most
of those elegant sites blur in my memory.

Because eventually, something happened. I'm not sure
either of us can pinpoint when we changed, but our worldview shifted. Our priorities, needs, and wants finally reached a
tipping point where our perspectives changed regarding what
was valuable to us.

As we continued listing the past venues where we had
celebrated our wonderful marriage, we noticed that instead of
waking up in luxury, we had begun waking up on our anniversary under mosquito netting in places like Mozambique, Ghana,
Honduras, and Haiti. Our exclusive restaurants were mud huts
and the gourmet menu was rice, beans, and goat meat. The
natural beauty of our surroundings began to outshine even the
most spectacularly decorated dining rooms. Instead of a string
quartet, our music consisted of tribal drums and the chirp of
insects.

Several years ago, we celebrated thirty-four years of marriage, this time in our new home. Our mosquito netting now permanently resides in Thomazeau, Haiti. Here we enjoy dining alfresco in the open-air concrete pavilion that has also doubles as a clinic and school for Live Beyond. We give special thanks for our facility's solar panels, clean running water, and septic tank. Barbecued chicken with fresh mangoes has permanently replaced veal marsala.

Now we know former slave children by name, share our food with hungry neighbors, and try to heal the sick and wounded on a daily basis. My surgical skills are now mixed with repairing generators, setting up water-purification systems, and providing medical care to the poorest of the poor. Sadly, sometimes we help bury the ones who lose the battle.

Laurie traded her comfortable life to run LiveBeyond's child nutrition program and our at-risk children programs. Her days are spent loving and caring for those clinging to the edge of life. Everyone adores her and she is called "Mama Laurie" by the Haitian children and adults alike. It thrills her to spend an afternoon going on home visits, moving from hut to hut delivering bags of food, blessing newborns, and bringing love to those in need.

And you know what the strangest thing of all has been? As our palates have lost their appetites for life's finer things, our lives have become richer than ever before. We have never experienced as much joy or felt as connected as we do in sharing what God has called us to do here in Haiti.

Each anniversary only brings more to celebrate.

—

Honestly, I'm not sure how to help you understand the shift that occurred in my heart. But the bottom line is that I discovered what God's divine economy is all about. You see, it's a very different kind of market than the one seen on Wall Street. It's still a market based on supply and demand, but perhaps it is better stated as being based on demand and supply.

Believe me when I say, where we live there is always a great demand. There's a demand for food, for clean water, for sanitation, for schools, for hospitals, for housing, for vitamins, for worm medications, for jobs, for the Gospel. I could go on and on. The demand is so great we've got great job security here!

And the supply—well, let me tell you about our supplier. He's got really, really deep pockets. In fact, He has more than we could ever dream of or imagine needing. He has more than we could ever ask for. And He already knows our needs before we even make a request.

Another great aspect of the Kingdom economy is the high rate of return on investment. Sometimes the rewards come at the very moment the investment is made. (That's rarely seen on Wall Street.) And yet the returns continue to be rolled over and increased throughout eternity.

The Kingdom economy isn't always based on actual financial currency, but a lot of times it is. At the time of this writing, the Haitian gourde has a conversion rate with the U.S. dollar of about 96 gourdes to 1 dollar. But not only can our United States dollars be converted into Haitian gourdes or Mexican pesos or Swiss francs, they can also be converted into Kingdom currency. In fact, the U.S. dollar has a pretty amazing conversion rate in the Kingdom of God.

At our LiveBeyond offices in Texas, there's a photo I had enlarged hanging in the hallway. It shows eight orphaned

Haitian boys gathered under a piece of rusty tin. If you look closely, you can see the edge of a river of sewage that runs right in front of the little shack they called home. When we encountered them, they had no adult guardians, no clean water, and only sporadic meals provided by the Red Cross. These little guys were on their own, surviving day to day as best they could.

Not that I could ever forget them, but I like having their picture to remind me of how I felt the first time I saw them.

There are roughly three hundred thousand orphans in Haiti, with the majority of them homeless. Many are sick from drinking contaminated water, and most are malnourished and slowly starving. We can't save every one of them, but that's never going to stop me from trying.

Laurie has always taken a special interest in children, particularly children in need. On so many of our home visits, our groups end up surrounded with curious, often malnourished children. The more we got to know these children, the more we realized just how close to death they might be. These children were dirty, stunted, and often on the brink of starvation. If they didn't receive a significant meal within the next few weeks, they were not going to survive. Many of them had not been attending school.

These children were destined to be economic orphans, living on the streets because their families couldn't provide for all of their needs. Or worse, some would be sold as a "restavèk," the term for child slaves in Haiti. Restavèks are household slaves forced to perform tasks with little or no restitution. Often they are victims of physical and sexual abuse, and as they have no way to remove themselves from their situation, they endure their hardships in silence or take to the streets.

The sad thing is that most families who sell their children into slavery believe that they are providing a better life for their children. These are typically poor rural families, living well below the poverty line, without the resources to provide for their ever-growing families. They believe that the new owners of their child will provide schooling, food, and even job opportunities that these children could never reach from their home communities. They believe that a life in slavery is better than the life they are living in poverty. And while there are cases of restavèks with owners who do fulfill their promises, many of these children are abandoned and left without hope.

With the children in our own community in mind, LiveBeyond began the "Kè Pou Timoun" program in 2015. Kè Pou Timoun means "Heart for Children" in Haitian Creole. We intended to limit the program to no more than 30 children, but by the end of the first week, we were pushing 50. Each of these children were at least 40 percent underweight for their age. This type of malnutrition can lead to developmental delays, educational challenges, and can even make children more susceptible to disease by weakening their immune system. Now we have over 150 of these children in our program. These children receive two meals per day—one through the program and one through school, which we provide through a partnership with Convoy of Hope. We pay the fees for their enrollment in school and offer tutoring, ESL lessons, Bible lessons, leadership training, and other fun activities. In 2017, 100 percent of the children in the program were enrolled in school. And in 2018 we opened our own school for about 100 children. Laurie and our education team ensure that this school runs at high standards so that we can prepare the children in our area for success. During the summer, a group of hard-working

American college students hosts a summer camp full of science experiments, sports activities, Bible studies, water games, and various learning opportunities. It has been amazing to see the transformation of the children in the program in terms of weight gained, inches grown, and higher grade letters earned. The parents of the children in our program are happy that their children have a safe place to be off the streets, extra food, and additional educational assistance. Many of them hope their younger children can enter the program, too, when they come of age. Our Haitian staff who run the program are well trained and enthusiastic about the work they are doing for the future of Haiti.

This program is not just your run-of-the-mill afterschool program. It is an orphan prevention and anti-restavèk program. Many of these children are able to stay with their families because of the support we can provide through our generous donors. The number of children who have not entered into slavery due to this program is immeasurable. It is our hope that we can continue to provide a way out for the families in our community as long as the need exists.

One little girl always comes to the front of my mind when I think about the successes of this program. Cherline has had the prefix "ti," meaning "little" or "small" in Haitian Creole, attached to her name for as long as I can remember. When we first met TiCherline, she was tiny, even compared to her malnourished peers. Her parents died before we met her, so she has been raised by her loving, but very elderly grandparents. In fact, it is she who does most of the caregiving in this situation. It takes no stretch of the imagination to know that her grandparents were probably tempted at some point to sell her to make ends meet.

In 2015 when she entered the program, she and her little brother were far below the 40 percent underweight standards we had set for entry into the program, and neither had ever been to school. But there was a light in TiCherline's eyes that let everyone around her know that her fierce spirit would not be quenched. Her smile is contagious. Americans and Haitians alike can't help but be drawn to her overwhelming charisma. She is full of spunk and that indefinable electricity present in many world leaders. There is just something special about TiCherline that I don't even want to imagine losing to the oppression of malnutrition.

TiCherline is still small for her age, as is her brother, but their growth rates have changed dramatically. Malnutrition, thankfully, took nothing from TiCherline's mind. In fact, she is currently at the top of her class. I still remember staring in amazement at her grades as Mama Laurie brought in the report cards for that day. A girl who was prevented by extreme poverty from even attending school is three years later at the top of her class! Laurie and I both practically danced with joy at the transformation of this little girl. And her brother is walking in his big sister's shoes!

I have no problems imagining TiCherline as the second female president of Haiti. It doesn't take much to make a big difference in a child's life. Because the genius of God's economy is that He gives earthly wealth in order to expand His eternal Kingdom.

What a mystery! The Great Supplier uses material resources to affect the spiritual realm. He actually stocks His people with all the necessary goods to meet the physical needs of people in the earthly domain in order to bless them in the Heavenly sphere.

Our role in this economy is to be a useful conduit for His supplies. All of the supplies come from Him. It's all from God. Even the ability to work and earn money comes from Him. "Remember the Lord your God, for it is He who gives you the ability to produce wealth" (Deuteronomy 8:18).

Do you hear that? *How* do we make money? We make money because God gives us the ability. It's not because we are smart or good-looking. It's not because we have a good business model or a phenomenal talent. It is because God *gives* us the power. God, the great Provider, the Supplier, gives *us* the ability to make money.

Scripture is equally clear on *why* we make money—and it's not to *acquire* wealth. Of course, we need to work in order to eat, to make a home, to take care of our families as well as those in need. You see, God is not opposed to wealth. He is, in fact, the source of all wealth.

The problem lies not in making money. The problem lies in keeping it for ourselves.

The purpose of our wealth is to be a funnel of blessings for others.

Do we believe that? Do we use our income to advance God's kingdom and to invest in matters of eternal significance? Or do we spend most of it on ourselves? Do we know that when we are given the *ability* to make money, we've been given the *responsibility* to care for not only our own basic needs but also the basic needs of others?

Scripture is crystal clear about the siren call of wealth. God knows the temptation of riches, and He warns us, saying, "Those who want to get rich fall into temptation and a trap and into many foolish and harmful desires that plunge people into ruin and destruction. For the love of money is a root of all kinds of evil. Some people, eager for money, have wandered from the faith and pierced themselves with many griefs" (1 Timothy 6:9–10).

Even though it's easy for us to look at those who are wealthy and recognize their propensity to dysfunction, the church is still filled with people whose hearts are set on wealth and social prominence, hoping to share the lifestyle of the rich and famous while thinking they can avoid their troubles.

I have watched many of my childhood friends follow their parents on the road of fame and fortune, only to reach the pinnacle of their profession yet end up leading desperate lives, several even committing suicide. It seems counterintuitive. Why would a person who has everything this world can offer still be unhappy? Why would someone with the ability to go where he wants, when he wants, and buy what he wants think his life isn't worth living?

The answer is that there is nothing in this world that can satisfy the needs of our heart. Only God can quench our needs. Only His work can bring satisfaction. Only His path leads to love, significance, and eternal peace.

God blesses us with material wealth for one reason: to be conduits of His abundance for those around us.

Now, *that* is the Kingdom economy.

CHAPTER 14

"JEZI SE SENYE!" (JESUS IS LORD!)

To live beyond means to be open to the Spirit's convicting power.

A FEW YEARS AGO, I NOTICED THAT ONE OF OUR DONORS, AN older, wealthy oilman from Texas, had not renewed the contribution he had made for several years. While there were reasons why he might have chosen not to continue giving, I knew this man well enough to pick up the phone and have an honest conversation with him.

"David," he said after our pleasantries were exchanged, "I won't beat around the bush. You know I think the world of you and Laurie and admire what the Lord has called you to do there in Haiti ..."

"Thank you, sir," I said, "that means a lot ... *but* ..."

"But I just don't know if I should continue pouring money into a country that's had billions of dollars invested with little to no return. I grew up listening to my parents and grandparents talk about what it was like in the Great Depression. Everyone was hurtin', but everybody got by somehow. And you know why?"

I saw where he was going but played along. "Why?"

"Because they *had to*," he drawled. "They had no choice. There weren't welfare and government assistance and church ministries and world relief organizations. Our parents knew that if they didn't do for themselves, nothin' would change! Seems to me that maybe if the Haitian people didn't have people givin' 'em food and medicine and money, then they'd learn to work, to change, to grow. Am I wrong to think this way?"

"I think I understand what you're saying," I replied. I'd heard this kind of pull-yourself-up-by-your-bootstraps logic before and had even subscribed to it myself for quite some time. "And I totally agree that everyone should do their part. The Bible says if you don't work, then you don't eat. That's what Paul told the Thessalonians." (2 Thessalonians 3:10)

"Yes, he did!" my friend said as if I'd just proven his point. But I wasn't done yet.

"But I also know firsthand a lot of these people can't work—they're crippled, they're sick, they are orphans and widows. They have no families to care for them and no one to help them with life's basic necessities. Most of these people have never been to school. They've never even known anyone who has gone to college. They live twenty miles from the city of Port-au-Prince but have never been there. They ride a donkey if they ride anything at all. They use the bathroom behind a bush. They drink from a stream. Their children die from ear infections, and they spend their lives in fear of a Voodou priest putting a curse on them." I paused to let that sink in. "Jesus was just as clear when He told us whoever gives a cup of water in His name was doing it as if He were the one in need. Add that to all those passages that talk about taking care of each other, especially those who can't take care of themselves—well, I think God wants all of us to obey those instructions."

There was only silence from the other end of the phone for a few long seconds. "I just don't know, David," he said, "maybe I should pray on it some more."

· "I think that's a great idea," I said, and, suddenly inspired, added, "and I'd ask you to pray about this: before you donate another penny to LiveBeyond, I'd love for you to come down and visit us in Thomazeau. It's not the Ritz, but we'll show you firsthand what we're doing and how we're doing it. Would you be willing to pray about coming down to visit us?"

He laughed and said, "You're really good at this, David. Yeah, I'll pray, and I'll probably come down there to see for myself what I suspect is true. But don't think holding sick babies and looking into the eyes of orphans is going to make me feel any differently."

"Fair enough," I said, saying a prayer of my own. "You know I appreciate all you've already done for us. And I'd love to have you come to visit. Thank you for your honesty just now. I look forward to hearing from you."

We said our goodbyes, and I figured that was that.

I'm convinced the only way to bring about lasting change in Haiti is to bring about spiritual rebirth. My friend had valid points, and I knew I would never convince him by arguing facts and figures and trying to explain the psyche of the Haitian culture—something I'm not sure I could begin to articulate. That's why I invited him down to see for himself. God would have to melt his heart through his encounters with people.

———

A big smile spread across my face as I scanned the list of volunteers who would be joining us for a week in Thomazeau a few months later. My old friend from Texas was listed. Considering the last conversation we'd had, I was definitely surprised. But I've also learned never to underestimate what God's Spirit can do in terms of moving the human heart. I had to give my friend credit for being willing to come for he did, indeed, follow through with his intention.

Sure enough, a couple weeks later, Laurie and I greeted him, welcoming him to the Hamilton Guesthouse on our LiveBeyond base in Thomazeau. Our Haitian staff and many children from our *Hearts for Children* program have a welcoming tradition by gathering and singing whenever a new crew of volunteers arrives for a visit. You don't have to understand Haitian Creole, a beautiful language descended from a blending French with West African tribal dialects, to feel the warm welcome being extended. It's enough to make any Southerner proud.

I sat with my friend that evening at dinner, a delicious meal of bean and chicken stew over rice with slaw, fresh tomatoes, and avocados. We've been fortunate to hire some wonderful Haitian women to cook for the LiveBeyond team. Already fine cooks, they received further training to ensure sanitary standards and to make the most of our limited ingredients. My friend ate with relish and seemed relaxed as we enjoyed the breeze in the open-air pavilion that serves as our dining hall.

"How was the drive in from Port-au-Prince?" I asked him.

He laughed and said, "A man could get rich here selling tires and shocks! I've never seen so many potholes, craters, and off-road conditions. Even in the city, you couldn't go more than a few yards before the pavement ends. Asphalt, gravel, dirt road, then nothing. And don't even get me started about the way we had to dodge the donkeys, goats, and chickens. I just knew we were going to run over a dog when we swerved around a pig."

"Yeah," I said, "there wasn't much of a highway system to start with, but the earthquake pretty much wiped out the roads along with everything else."

We continued to chat about the week ahead. Maybe he was just exhausted from the flight and then that rocky drive, but my old friend seemed warmer and softer than when we talked a couple of months earlier on the phone.

We didn't get to talk much in the hectic days that followed. More people than usual lined up to be seen in our clinic, and our volunteers were stretched to their limits. The couple of times I did see my friend, he was either holding a baby or pouring water into Dixie cups and handing it out to people suffering under the hot tropical sun. I continued praying that when he looked into the eyes of the hurting, he would see Jesus. And while I'm sure God answered my prayer throughout that entire week, I suspect one particular home visit tipped the scale.

We had navigated the deep ruts of the La Hatte road many times before on our way to visit the infirm residents living in the baked-mud huts dotting the thorny countryside. That day we had a little caravan of trucks with volunteers holding on as they rode in the truck beds. Going slowly, we forced our unwilling tires over the ancient rocks and through the deep brown water as we passed exhausted women who balanced baskets on their heads and yanked their obdurate donkeys home from the market.

Clouds of mosquitos and flies swarmed as our tires disturbed their breeding pools in stagnant puddles, a graphic reminder for us all to be sure to take our anti-malarial medication that night and apply a fresh coat of mosquito repellent. Without the usual refreshing breeze to disperse them, it seemed as though each of these buzzing insects was intent on sharing its deadly malaria parasite with us. A huge black sow soaked in the coolness of the wallow in the center of our road, forcing us to redirect our wheels. As we turned our battered trucks to miss the massive beast, we saw him.

A pair of wild eyes peered at us from the side of a sun-baked mud house beyond the road. They did not look particularly happy to see us. Always expecting the unexpected, I prayed that we would not face resistance or encounter violence that afternoon.

The area of Thomazeau where we found ourselves, called Pont Batay, is on the edge of a vast salt flat, presumably left behind by a retreating ancient Caribbean ocean. What the sea creatures abandoned was now a desolate, salt-encrusted wasteland inhabited by an oppressed group of people. The white-bleached countryside reflected the vacuous hopelessness of the residents.

This was a place filled with Voodou.

Local lore claims that the people of Pont Batay "love the devil very much." Surrounded by several Voodou peristyles and even a Voodou community center, this village is undoubtedly dominated by evil spirits. In fact, the name *Pont Batay* means "Bridge of Fighting." The enemy had fought here, and it seemed to us that he was winning the fight.

As we drove closer, the wild-eyed man continued to glare at us. Tall and reed thin, his one-hundred-forty pounds gripped his six-foot-four frame like a wetsuit. But it was his eyes that were so startling. They glowed with a primal fear that was unmistakable. As our little caravan came to a full stop in front of his home, he bared his teeth and hissed at us like a giant serpent rising up from the ground.

His hissing and snarling continued as we began to dismount our vehicles and slowly walk towards him. As he lunged forward at the closest of us, he raised his hands in an anguished attempt to scare us off. It was then that everyone saw his hands. They were bound with coarse hemp ropes.

Just then an old Haitian woman emerged from the house and spoke sharply to the man as if calling down a barking dog. Laurie greeted her and introduced her to the Americans who had come to visit. This wonderful lady, so burdened with the hardships of caring for her family, went to each visitor and kissed them on the cheek. With nothing concrete to offer, her form of hospitality was her genuinely genteel welcome.

While she was greeting her visitors, three more Haitian men came and sat down on the front steps of the house, next to Laurie. One had a withered hand and spoke in the singsong voice of a child. Another kept his hand on the waist of his pants to keep them from falling down because they were at least six sizes too big for him. His eyes were not focused, and his feeble smile denoted that he could not comprehend much of his surroundings, but he, too, sat down on the steps. The third man flashed his toothless grin and hungrily reached for the peanut butter crackers Laurie had brought along.

Eventually, all the family sat down except for the first man we had seen. He continued to stand and hiss whenever anyone approached. Laurie reached up, grabbed his arm, and pulled him to sit down beside her. She explained that Ramon was the grandson of our gracious hostess. His hands were bound in order to keep him from harming his family or himself during his frequent violent outbursts. Now he shook his bound hands at us in the anger inspired uniquely by the enemy.

According to local beliefs, Ramon was cursed and possessed by an evil spirit. While I knew that the enemy was exploiting this poor man, I also knew that he likely suffered from having a mental or physical handicap, or both. In Haiti, there is no government system of support for the mentally or physically disabled. They are left to their own devices with family members who are often unable or unwilling to care for them. In Ramon's case, his grandmother did her best to provide for him and the other men who had joined us.

This is a home that we visit regularly as part of our At Risk program. The program is targeted toward meeting the needs of the old, disabled, and weak in our society. Our Haitian staff informs us of people in need in their villages, and we reach out to offer medical care, nutritional support, and friendship. While we know that the basics of life like food and medicines are needed, we want to bring the real life of Jesus to those in need. Laurie always sits on the steps with the family, singing Haitian songs and praying. On this day, she felt inspired to make declarations about the Truth of God. She wanted all in the spiritual realm to hear the Truth being spoken in this evil-infested village.

"Jezi bon!" (Jesus is good!), Laurie said. "Jezi bon!" the family repeated. But Ramon hissed.

"Jezi fò!" (Jesus is powerful!), Laurie continued. "Jezi fò!" all echoed but one.

Laurie gave her favorite line. "Jezi ap veni!" (Jesus is coming!) Four voices cried out.

"Jezi se Senye!" (Jesus is Lord!) All five people looked at Laurie. First of all, the grandmother repeated, "Jezi se Senye," then the hungry one said, "Jezi se Senye." Slowly, the singsong voice said, "Wi, Jezi se Senye" followed by a faraway whisper, "Jezi se Senye."

Laurie turned and looked hard at Ramon. His fierce glare softened, and he hung his head. She repeated, "Jezi se Senye."

We all held our breaths and waited. Slowly Ramon raised his head, nodded to the sky, and said in a clear voice, "Oui, Jezi se Senye." (Yes, Jesus is Lord.)

I know the earthquake hit Port-au-Prince in 2010, but something shook the earth in Pont Batay on this day. Everyone broke out into cheers. The true King had been acknowledged. The true Lord of Heaven and Earth had been declared. Only Jesus is Lord, and even Ramon had to admit His authority. For "no one can say 'Jesus is Lord,' except by the Holy Spirit." (1 Corinthians 12:3b)

When it was finally time for us to leave Ramon and his family that day, I watched as my old friend from Texas reached his hand out toward Ramon and began to pray.

Later he told me that he had never felt more alive.

He's now returned three times to Thomazeau and takes a personal interest in visiting his friend Ramon on each visit. He is, once again, a very supportive donor to LiveBeyond's programs.

All this because one Texan went beyond his own politics and prejudices and opened himself to the convicting power of the Holy Spirit.

Time and again I've seen how my own efforts to convince people to give generously would fall flat if not for the saving grace and convicting efforts of the Holy Spirit. Sometimes I get so overwhelmed by the needs I see all around me, so dismayed at the wealth I witness on my trips back to the States, so horrified and angered at the injustice of it all. But that's when I remember that it is the Holy Spirit that is moving people, not me. While the Lord uses me, He is the one to actually change people's hearts to give and sacrifice for my friends in Haiti.

It was this convicting power that brought me to Haiti in the first place.

It was this convicting power that kept me coming back.

And it was this power that convinced me that I should give up my comfortable life in the United States to live and serve in Haiti full time. It broke me out of living a life of ease so that I could learn how to be a conduit of His abundance in the Kingdom. May we all submit to His convicting power when we are asked!

CHAPTER 15

ONCE YOU KNOW THEIR NAMES

*To live beyond means to extend
yourself on behalf of others.*

FOLLOWING JESUS'S EXAMPLE TRANSFORMS US FROM BEING bystanders in the Kingdom to being actively involved in the building of His Kingdom on earth. We want to live out the Lord's Prayer, making His Kingdom come and His will be done here on earth, as it is in Heaven. After we moved to Haiti, Laurie and I, along with our small team, began ministering to as many people as possible. Word quickly spread through the surrounding villages, and occasionally a local would burst into our clinic begging us to help with their medical emergency.

One sultry afternoon, an older man came rushing through our gates, clearly in distress. Through sobs, he haltingly stammered that his daughter was dying in a village not far from our base. Unsure of her exact location or condition, we launched up the mountain in our four-wheel-drive truck with a trauma kit that we hoped would be sufficient.

Soon we came to a barely visible goat path that marked the way to Claudia's house. We parked the truck as closely as we could to the head of the trail and picked our way through the thorn-covered bushes that led to the village of Jacasse.

Our daughter, Jacklyn, saw her first. She was lying prostrate in the dirt, the hot Caribbean sun assaulting her fragile body. Starvation sapped the last of the girl's vitality. As we rushed to her aid, her sunken eyes and thready pulse told the story of her impending demise from chronic malnutrition. Too weak to recognize our presence, the girl barely moved. Jacklyn held her, hoping to resuscitate what was left of her emaciated body.

"What is her name?" Jacklyn asked.

"Claudia," a nearby child murmured.

As a crowd of villagers gathered, we learned that two years before, this then-vibrant eighteen-year-old girl shopped in the market five miles distant and dreamed of breaking free of her desperate surroundings. One day, though, she complained of an earache, which, untreated in her resource-poor environment, progressed to what we assume was meningitis. When it finished its punishing devastation, Claudia was left partially paralyzed and debilitated.

Claudia's family told us that she had once lived with and served her grandfather by shopping for him and gathering water and firewood. After the death of Claudia's mother, her father went to the grandfather's house to bring Claudia home to serve him. In his jealous anger, the grandfather put a Voodou curse on Claudia and told her dad, "You can have her, but she won't be any good to you." Shortly thereafter, Claudia became sick and the grandfather's evil prediction came true. The Voodou worshipers pronounced her accursed and compelled the people to shun her. Rejected, immobile, and alone, Claudia was left as a pariah to slowly starve. The poorest girl in the poorest village in the poorest country in the Western Hemisphere was demonized and sullied by her neighbors.

Claudia's eyes opened briefly in response to Jacklyn's efforts to revive her, so Jacklyn turned to clean the feces and vomit from Claudia's soiled body. Jacklyn implored Claudia's aunt to regularly wash and feed her and we offered her father a job on our base so that he could have sufficient income to buy her food.

It's with this girl that Jacklyn learned the secret to building God's kingdom: *she learned her name.* No longer was Jacklyn just taking care of a poor Haitian girl. She was taking care of Claudia. She knew Claudia's name. She couldn't stop thinking of Claudia, praying for Claudia, devising ways to ensure care for Claudia.

I like to tell our team members, "Once you know their names, there's no going back."

We don't participate in the economy building of the Kingdom of God because it's commanded. We participate because we're compelled. Love should compel us to extend ourselves on behalf of others so that those like Claudia may become rich.

The Scripture comes to life: "For you know the grace of our Lord Jesus Christ, that though he was rich, yet for your sake, he became poor so that you through His poverty might become rich" (2 Corinthians 8:9). To truly live beyond, we must live the reality of God's Word and make it look like something. Jacklyn realized she must insert her name for Jesus's name and Claudia's name for her own. For Jacklyn then, it reads like this: "For you know the grace of Jacklyn Vanderpool, that though she was rich, yet for Claudia's sake, Jacklyn became poor so that by her poverty, Claudia might become rich." When Jacklyn graduated from college, she was offered several jobs in the United States. But she chose, instead, to move to Haiti to live with us so that she could serve people like Claudia. She chose a negligible salary, a stressful work environment, and a life of restriction so that she could help Claudia and others like her have a better life. She willingly sacrificed for others to advance the Kingdom.

Each of us can do this. The question is, how much do we really want to be like Jesus? He left the ultimate gated community in Heaven to live as a poor Jewish man under the subjection of the Roman government so that everyone, including people who lorded power over Him, could have an abundant life. And He willingly made this sacrifice and became poor so that all of us could become rich. If we want to be like Him, we will do what He did.

I suggest you try this exercise. For whom are you willing to become poor? Maybe someone in your family. But what about someone else? Do you know and love someone enough to be willing to do this? Can you say, "For you know the grace of [your name], that though He was rich, for [other person's name]'s sake [your name] became poor so that [other person's name] might become rich."

What a life-changing statement! What a world-changing attitude! This is the way we live like Jesus. This is how we transform others. This is the way we live beyond. This is the way we participate in the Kingdom economy—we become poor so that others may become rich.

If we all join the amazing economy of the Kingdom in building God's kingdom here on earth, all the Claudias of the world will have life and have life abundantly, both here on earth and someday in Heaven. This is the radical call of Jesus to change the way we deal with our time, talents, money, connections, and resources. We are no longer bystanders in the kingdom. We become the conduits of God's grace. His grace becomes the essence of our lives. And as we pour out His grace, extending ourselves on behalf of others, their names will be written not only on our hearts but may someday be revealed etched in the eternal Book of Life.

Our grace, *our poverty*, results in eternal wealth for the world.

About three years after we found Claudia, her body finally succumbed to the illnesses that ravaged her body for so long. By then, because of the efforts of Jacklyn and many other volunteers who served her, Claudia knew love. She knew what it felt like to be clean and fed and comfortable and safe. Her father and siblings realized her worth as a family member. Most importantly, Jesus was spoken over her every day for the rest of her life. We are confident that she is fully restored to health in Heaven with Jesus.

Jacklyn continues her work through the various programs of LiveBeyond. As her father, I am so proud of how the Lord uses her because of her willingness to extend herself on behalf of others.

Whose name is on your heart? For whom are you willing to become poor?

CHAPTER 16

GOD'S CHILD

To live beyond means to reach out to those
who are abandoned by society.

IT HAD BEEN A HARD DAY AND IT WAS ABOUT TO BECOME HARDER.

The relentless Haitian sun was completing its course above the desolate landscape as our LiveBeyond team put the finishing touches on our latest water-purification system. We were in a community of homes on the outskirts of Thomazeau. Mud huts, worse than most in the developing world, were interspersed with shacks of tin and plywood and a few concrete houses, built by long-gone NGOs. The cracked mud of the road and houses reflected the pasty-white saline dust frequently blowing in the tropical breeze.

We were in a dry plain, a barren salt pan of desert-like ground that extended the width of the narrowly separated mountains. While we were providing access to clean water to the people living in this fractured countryside, this area proved especially difficult. A salty film covered everything, including the water, and we struggled to render it drinkable.

The people of this area matched their salty surroundings and were contesting us as well. A group of young men ruled the neighborhood in the same fashion as an inner-city gang. They tolerated our presence, but we soon discovered their stares veiled a terrible secret.

———

A tiny figure flitted several hundred feet away at the periphery of our mobile clinic/work area. Unsure if what we had just seen was real or a figment of our imagination due to dehydrated brains, a small group of our mobile medical team walked over and peered curiously behind the crumbling, bleached hut to look closer. Covered in white dirt, hair matted with salt and dung, a scowling face with piercing eyes atop an angular three-foot frame squinted back at us.

At first, none of us could tell if she was a woman or a child. More unsettling than her appearance, though, was the feral grunting coming from her snarled lips. Was this a Voodou curse or a primal greeting? We couldn't tell if these sounds represented a warning not to come too close or were a cry for help. Hoping for the latter but prepared for the former, we warily approached.

She continued to growl and snarl as a member of our Haitian staff attempted communication. There in the shadows, we could see her face, a woman of indeterminable age. She could have been twelve or sixty; we simply couldn't tell because of the dirt, mud, and excrement obscuring her face. As we heard her neighbors talking loudly among themselves, the situation became clearer.

Just then a girl of nine or ten, wearing a man's gray T-shirt as a dress, stepped in front of us. She was a spectator coming to see what all the fuss was about. A staff member spoke to her, asking about the woman in front of us. The girl shrugged, said the woman's name was Corrine, and said that she was cursed—an animal.

Voodou dictates the banishment of those who are defective. People with mental, physical, or emotional differences are not typically welcomed in the ranks of the "acceptable." The term used for anyone with disabilities or handicaps is "kokobay," meaning worthless. Abandoned by their families and without caretakers of any kind or a government welfare system, these individuals are often treated worse than animals. Like their neighbors, they lack clean water and functioning sewers, but these castaways are also forced to dwell where they can find any kind of refuge—including pigpens, like Corrine.

It is beyond inhumane, and the situation we saw that day enraged me. This woman, dwarf in stature and contorted by some kind of spinal deformity, had been locked in a single-room hut with swine and forced to exist in the muddy wallows littered with excrement.

Her real deprivation was most likely nutritional. Obviously, she had been forced to survive on plant husks, uncooked grains, and whatever scraps of spoiled food that might have been thrown into her shed. Outcasts in similar situations slowly starve as the hogs best their attempts at eating the garbage, wasting away until they become nourishment for the hogs themselves.

Now fueled by compassion and no longer alarmed, we made our way inside. Corrine began jabbering, clearly agitated and unsure of our motive. I've never seen a more touching moment than when one of our female volunteers, Natasha, boldly stepped forward with tears in her eyes and gently began wiping away the dirt from Corrine's face. The small woman resisted at first but eventually allowed Natasha to wipe her face clean.

Neighbors began to gather to watch what they considered nothing more than a circus sideshow. The gang who terrorized the village began to walk our way as well.

"Anyone have an energy bar or food?" Natasha asked. "She needs something to drink too."

I carefully began to examine Corrine for wounds or injuries. Only three feet tall, her twisted body was wrenched forward and side-to-side by the cruel combined grip of scoliosis and lordosis. Unknown prenatal forces had so twisted her pliable spine that without corrective surgery, she was destined to live in constant pain.

Loud chatter and angry shouts began to fill the air around us, and I didn't need our fine Haitian staff to help me understand their message. A few of Corrine's neighbors began to throw rocks and chunks of dried mud our way.

Our attempts to feed Corrine were met with distrust from her and ridicule from the growing crowd. This woman had lived so long without the kindness of human touch that she feared we were only there to join her neighbors in their continuous torment. A member of our Haitian staff purchased some cheese crackers with his own money to give to Corrine. We later found out that the vendor of those crackers was Corrine's sister, hardened to the plight of her relative. Natasha, now joined by Laurie, continued to sing softly and held out a handful of Haitian cheese crackers. Corrine looked cautiously at the bright orange snack, and her hunger overcame her fear.

She feverishly grabbed the crackers from Natasha's hand and shoved them deep into her mouth. I was afraid she was going to choke on her hand with how far she drove it down her throat. She guzzled a Powerade-filled Nalgene bottle Laurie offered. The crowd grew more raucous, with the gang obviously upset by the kindness being shown to someone they constantly bullied. To shelter Corrine from the sticks and insults thrown at her, our small group huddled closer around her.

We cringed to think of how long she had suffered this way. Our hearts crumbled when we learned she was forty-two years old.

Corrine's fear continued to recede as her hunger and thirst were abated. Though clearly uncommunicative, her mind seemed alert as she purposely shuttled from one heart-wrenched American to another, gorging on whatever snacks their hands held. Something in her eyes made me wonder about her level of awareness.

Was her condition a result of a genetic defect like osteogenesis imperfecta, or had she been so severely isolated from human contact that her speech patterns were shaped by the grunts and squeals of the pigs sharing her sty? Whatever the cause, Corrine needed a voice.

As our battered little team finally drove away in speechless silence, we watched in mounting anger as Corrine was chased around the desolate village, her food stolen, and her precious water given to the goats. As the darkness fell on that unholy village, we knew the job we were called to do.

Several years later, our attempts to help have barely rejuvenated Corrine. We are thwarted by a family member who sees our compassion for Corrine as a meal ticket for himself, and he refuses to let us give her continual care. However, previously wary of our help, Corrine now becomes animated and excited at our arrival. Most times we still find her trapped in with the pigs, and she's always covered with dirt, wearing the same clothes we'd put on her during our previous visit.

Most of her neighbors still take delight in the maleficent entertainment provided at the expense of the unwanted Americans focusing so much attention on this allegedly unworthy, broken woman. They refuse to realize that she is just as much God's child as they are. They refuse to realize that we are all just as needy as Corrine.

———

Unfortunately, Voodou worshipers aren't the only people who make outcasts of those who are different. A person doesn't have to be as disfigured as Corrine and live in a pigpen in order to suffer cruel treatment and social disenfranchisement. It seems to be part of our fallen human nature to seek comfort and security through similar, homogeneous people. We like being with people who are like ourselves. The other is, well, other.

Laurie's family has dealt with this type of injustice for more than half a century. In 1962, her little brother, John Mark Stallings, was born with Down syndrome. At the time of his birth, the only advice that Coach and my mother-in-law, Mrs. Ruth Ann, received was to put Johnny in an institution. They were warned that raising a child with such a handicap would spell the end of coaching opportunities and would mar the lives of their other children. In direct defiance of all counsel, Coach and Mrs. Ruth Ann determined to love Johnny and give him the life that they would want for any son of theirs. Their story is beautifully told in Coach's book *Another Season*.

One of my greatest blessings in life was to know and love Johnny. Because of the way he was raised, loved, and adored by his parents and four sisters, the attitudes of parents throughout America were changed toward people with Down syndrome. The Stallings willingly used the national platform of athletics to showcase the pleasures awarded to families of people with Down's.

We named our own son John Mark in honor of Johnny. Our John Mark grew up with a sense that he was distinguished with this special gift. Especially close to Johnny, John Mark developed a sensitivity to injustice. Sensitivity does not mean softness. No one who's ever been around John Mark Vanderpool would describe him as soft. He has a unique mixture of physical toughness and spiritual discipline that sets him apart. Woe to the man who brings injustice to the weak. John Mark relishes the role of linebacker for the vulnerable. Just as he stalked his prey on the football fields in Tennessee, he stalks the backwoods of Haiti, searching for those who need a defender, a voice, a shelter.

One of the ways many people see John Mark's sensitivity is through his relationship with Widler. When we first met Widler, he was among the children at Bobby's orphanage.

Widler was not a true orphan but an orphan of circumstances. He was abandoned by his father, and his mother's new husband did not want to raise him with his own children, so he was left to the care of Bobby's orphanage. After several years, through lots of prayers, Bobby was able to facilitate Widler's transition to living with his mother and her husband amicably. Widler quickly learned English and became a favorite among the American team members. He bonded closely with John Mark and his wife, Lauren. So closely, in fact, that Widler gave them one of his family's goats as a wedding present. All because John Mark cared so deeply for this abandoned but lovable young man. John Mark poured into Widler, and Widler, out of the love in his heart, gave John Mark the biggest present he could in return.

Jesus Himself set an example of searching out those abandoned by society. The pregnant, unmarried mother. (His very own mother!) The lowly working-class fisherman. The demon-possessed. The blind. The leper. The beggar. The adulterer. The Samaritan. The tax collector. The thief on the cross. All people that were shunned, looked down upon, rejected. Yet Jesus sought them out, spoke with them, comforted them, challenged them, accepted them, taught them, discipled them, healed them.

Can we do any less?

At the heart of our outreach is the Johnny's Kids program. Named for Laurie's brother, Johnny's Kids now serves physically and mentally disabled children. We offer physical and occupational therapy, nutritional support, educational opportunities, and more. We hope to show the people of Thomazeau just how valuable these individuals are and just how much they can contribute to their communities.

Who do you see in your community who has been abandoned by society? The migrant worker, slaving in the hot fields? The refugee, scared and alone in a new country? The poor, stuck in crumbling neighborhoods and schools? The physically disabled, the senile, the mentally ill, the drug addict, the prisoner, the orphan, the widow, the ugly, the untalented, the friendless ... so many people crying out for love and for attention. To live beyond means to notice these people, to reach out to them, and to care.

Just like Jesus did.

CHAPTER 17

LIVE BEYOND FEAR

To live beyond means to push past doubt, fear, anxiety, and any other obstacle that would hold us back from acting on God's call on our lives.

In our first few years of living in Haiti, I would fly back to the States about once a quarter to meet with our team at the LiveBeyond offices in Tennessee and Texas. While there, I help coordinate schedules for medical professionals and other volunteers visiting us in Haiti, connect with various supporters and donors, and meet with other members of the LiveBeyond board of directors. It's always good to get back to the States and enjoy all that our country has to offer, but I definitely call Haiti my home. I always miss Laurie and my extended Haitian family of workers, students, and patients. Going between the two countries isn't culture shock as much as culture whiplash!

It's a bit surreal to go from seeing villagers riding donkeys and carrying jerry cans of water to seeing folks in sports cars drinking Evian. To go from the rubble roads, salt plains, and barren mountainsides of my adopted homeland to skyscrapers, landscaped lawns, and restaurants full of food sometimes makes me feel like an astronaut going back and forth between two very different planets.

Whenever I make these trips, I always wonder about what might go wrong back in Haiti—often for good reason. Haiti remains a dangerous place and where we live is quite remote. Riots and looting still occur both in urban neighborhoods, Port-au-Prince, and rural areas like ours. Because we feel a serious responsibility for all of our workers and volunteers, we have constructed a ten-foot-high concrete wall with concertina wire around the perimeter of our LiveBeyond base, and we have five guardhouses manned by security guards we've employed and trained.

Civil unrest, however, often leads to chaotic, sometimes violent demonstrations and riots. A shortage of gasoline might trigger such an uproar, or a new, unpopular government policy, or lack of follow-through on a prior political promise. We've grown accustomed to the sights and smell of burning tires and roadblocks, the favored tools of Haitian protests.

One such riot broke out while I was in Nashville. Sitting in a board meeting, with the other directors of LiveBeyond, we were expecting Laurie to join us via a Skype call. About fifteen minutes into the meeting, we hadn't heard from her, so I decided to give her a call. As she answered, I pressed the speaker-phone button and everyone gave her a warm welcome.

Immediately, I knew something was wrong. Jerking the phone up to my ear, I could barely hear my wife's voice above the raucous din of angry Haitian voices.

"David, can you hear me?" she said.

"Honey, what's wrong? Where are you? Are you okay?" I asked, bombarding her with questions.

"Honey, we've got a problem. We have a crowd, maybe a hundred or more at the front gate." Laurie's voice continued to compete with the noise around her.

"Get in the guesthouse!" I instructed. "Get the other staff women and lock yourselves in our bedroom. I'll call Jean-Phillipe" (our chief of security) "and have him get things under control."

"No, no!" she said, and her voice faded as I strained to hear. "I'm already out here. I'm outside the gate now. I had to get Jean-Phillipe myself. He was hiding inside the guardhouse and I pulled him out to come with me. The mob is trying to get one of our Haitian employees. There's been gunfire."

"Honey, get out of there and go in the house!" I said, trying not to let my panic seep through. Just then the roar of the crowd became so loud that I feared for her life. "Laurie!" I shouted.

"Hold on," she said calmly. Suddenly, the crowd's jeers stopped, and it became eerily quiet. I could barely hear Laurie's voice talking to someone, but it was clear she wasn't happy. I probably only waited about thirty or forty seconds, but it felt like days before my wife's voice came back on the line. I could hear talking and then a roar of loud voices.

"Well, you don't need to worry. It's under control," she said. "I'll call you back in a couple of hours, okay?"

"Wait!" I said. "What in the world just happened? Are you sure you're all right?"

"As I stood here," she said, "I asked the Lord to show me who had the pistol. Of all the people out here only one was sitting down. A man was squatting on the side of the hill trying to look nonchalant. I knew he was the one who had fired the shots. I walked over to him and demanded to see the weapon. He jumped up and ran away. The entire crowd broke into cheers as he ran. The leaders of the village chased him, and others assured me that all is fine now that he is gone. The crowd is dispersing. We're fine, David. You know I'm not the least bit afraid. I'll call you back later, okay? I love you, 'bye."

I wasn't sure whether to laugh, cry, fall to my knees in a prayer of thanksgiving, or all of the above. One thing the Haitians learn very quickly—and it sounded like some young buck had just found out the hard way—you shouldn't mess with "Mama Laurie"! For all her beauty, charm, and compassion, my wife is one tough lady.

"David?" One of the men from the meeting inquired. "Is everything okay? We sort of heard—and it sounded like—we can adjourn and reschedule if we need to."

"Everything's fine," I said, smiling. "Just my wife letting me know she's not going to tolerate riots in our front yard."

———

I don't want to minimize the danger that Laurie and our staff members faced that day. But afterward, I realized there aren't many scenarios that Laurie can't handle. She's not only my wife but also a true partner in every sense of the word, working tirelessly to love, feed, comfort, clothe, and educate her Haitian brothers and sisters. Anyone who knows her would never bet against her in a fight, but still, I remember how some friends and even family had responded when we told them we were moving to Haiti.

"Isn't it dangerous over there?" some of them asked. We acknowledged that it was.

"Aren't there all kinds of diseases and bacteria and viruses?" We agreed that Haiti has its share of factors facilitating certain diseases.

"And what do you expect to actually accomplish?"

"That's easy," my wife said. "We want to bring light to our region of Haiti—to help heal the people there, to see them come to know God, and to have them prepared for the return of the King, Jesus Christ."

Upon the arrival of each LiveBeyond team to our base, Laurie greets the new members. The road-weary Americans slowly make their way into the Hamilton guesthouse—generously funded by Tracie and Scott Hamilton, the 1980 Olympic gold medalist in figure skating—then out to our dining pavilion for their first Haitian feast. Along with exhaustion from the day's travels and the discombobulated feeling of being in unfamiliar surroundings, concern and anxiety often show on new guests' faces. We see them looking at the high walls with razor wire. We hear them talking about the fearful sights seen on the road from Port-au-Prince. It is at this time that Laurie gives her first speech.

"As you all know, Haiti is an inherently dangerous place," Laurie begins. "This is a country accustomed to violence, poisonings, curses, and death. We take your safety seriously and you will see our twenty-four-hour security guards throughout the base. Sometimes guests ask the question, 'What exactly should we be afraid of?' Let me tell you what you need to fear because you do need to be in fear. We invite you to join us in our fear."

At this point, there's a pause, sometimes accompanied by nervous glances. Laurie continues with a smile, "We walk in absolute fear of the Lord God Almighty. We fear Him and Him alone. As a result, we are afraid of nothing else."

The first time I heard Laurie say this, I thought, "Oh no. We're going to have people scared out of their wits." But just the opposite happened and continues to happen every time. A sense of peace settles over everyone. They realize that Something a lot more powerful than evil is present. They begin to see the Unseen, recognize His presence, and settle into His care.

The people who come to work alongside us in Haiti come because they refuse to be restricted by artificial limits caused by worry or self-protection. Some of the greatest barriers in life are self-imposed. We allow our apprehensions about these self-imposed hurdles to restrict what we are capable of doing. But the truth is that every human being encounters events over which they have no control. We all experience loss, heartache, grief, and disappointment. Everyone faces these challenges, but it is how we face these challenges that define who we are.

Don't get me wrong. Some challenges are not self-inflicted. These types of challenges may not be "overcome" or "defeated" in the traditional sense. These challenges are not what I'm talking about. I'm talking about the problems that we create for ourselves, the challenges that with the right means and opportunity we can rise above. I'm talking about the challenges that we can choose to live beyond in order to love others like Jesus.

The dangers in Haiti are not few and far between. They are many and often. They range from being bitten by a malaria-carrying mosquito to being caught in a violent mob. However, it makes me sad to hear too many of my friends say that they would love to come to serve on our LiveBeyond base, but they worry about getting sick or hurt. And I must admit that their worries are not entirely unfounded. In Haiti, I've experienced malaria, cholera, bed bugs, scabies, and death threats. On multiple occasions, I've had my car surrounded by a Haitian mob wanting bribes or jobs. It's not uncommon for us to have to get out of our vehicle and move the boulders that have been set out to block the road.

We've had ambushes planned against us. About a year after we moved to Haiti, as we were preparing to depart for the Port-au-Prince airport, we got a warning. Several villagers came to us and said that the dead bodies of two men were placed on the road. The murderers knew that we would be driving by, and they expected us to stop and give aid. The villagers warned us that this was an ambush. Sure enough, when we drove down the isolated road, we saw the bodies of two men who had been stoned to death. Because of the warning, we did not stop.

On another occasion, Laurie and I had been in the States fundraising for our child nutrition program and were finally heading home. We were thrilled to be heading back to Haiti since our fundraising efforts had been successful and we excitedly talked about how many more children we could feed with the money we had raised. As we talked on the last leg of our journey, I could tell that Laurie was unsettled. She said that she had a feeling something bad was about to happen but couldn't figure it out, so we prayed together as we bumped along the last miles that led to the LiveBeyond base.

The base was uncharacteristically dark as we entered suggesting that the generator system was down, so I initially went there to try to fix it. Oddly, I couldn't see any of our security guards we'd hired to guard the base. After an hour of working on the generator, I decided that we might need to spend the night in our hospital, which has a backup generator, so I asked Laurie to get some mattresses so we could sleep on the hospital floor. I continued working on the generator and thought I might be able to fix it if I had a different wrench.

As I walked around the north side of the guesthouse on my way to our cottage where I kept my toolbox, I heard Laurie scream. I ran as fast as I could towards the sound and came upon four armed men pistol-whipping Laurie and holding a knife to her neck. It seemed to me that time stopped as I saw my beautiful wife bleeding profusely from wounds to her face surrounded by men intent on killing her. I asked the Lord for strength and began yelling and swinging the heavy crescent wrench in my hand at her attackers.

Miraculously, they ran.

Laurie and I hurried to the guest house to assess her wounds and what I saw crushed me. My beautiful bride's face was badly beaten, and blood stained the front of her white shirt. Her back was black and blue, contused by the metal baton that had rained down on her without mercy, and her cheek was cut by their cruel machete.

Throughout it all, Laurie never shed a tear. As I gently washed her wounds and sutured her cuts—she smiled. Through that long night and the many long nights that followed, she never let fear overtake her; she knew that the Lord was her Shepherd, that He would lead her beside still waters, and He would restore her soul.

This terrible event changed us. Even though we had lived in Haiti two years by then and knew what we had sacrificed to serve God there, this was the first time that either of us had bled for our faith. Up to that time, we had sacrificed our wealth, our comfort, and our status but now Laurie had sacrificed her blood. Suddenly, the verse, "All who desire to live a Godly life will suffer persecution" came into focus. Then the verse, "Take up your cross daily and follow Me," was no longer a platitude quoted at church but actually became our new reality.

We had always known that our chosen profession was dangerous. We had discussed what we would do in case of an attack many times, and we had always had peace about the outcome. But now that we had been tested, would we respond well or turn our backs on bringing the Gospel to the Haitians? Many counseled us to leave, it was just too dangerous and besides, it wasn't worth it. As Laurie and I prayed and listened and searched the Scriptures for an answer, the Lord answered us.

They conquered him
by the blood of the Lamb
and by the word of their testimony,
for they did not love their lives
in the face of death.
Revelation 12:11 (HCSB)

I believe that Satan incited these men to attack Laurie and I believe that God gave me the strength to drive them away. If we retreated back to the States in the face of this trial, we would lose. If we stood tough and unafraid in the face of Satan's attack, we would win. Laurie now had a Satan-defeating testimony that, when coupled with the Blood of Jesus, always defeats the enemy.

The attacks continue and persecution doesn't stop. For many years the perpetrators were still at large and their attacks escalated. The lack of justice in Haiti meant that when this gang was arrested for their attack on Laurie, they "escaped" from prison after one day. They freely walked the streets of Haiti and regularly robbed our Haitian staff on payday. They routinely attacked our drivers, throwing rocks and breaking the windows of our trucks. These gangsters were the same men who later murdered our base manager, John Kely Garçon. These same men eventually kidnapped two of our staff managers, holding them for a terrible week of torture and threats. It was during this week that the Lord showed His mercy and delivered our area from evil. Not only were our staff managers released without ransom but the gangsters actually turned upon one another and while our godly workers were returned home, none of the gangsters survived the week. These men were Voodouists, they worshipped Satan and they persecuted Christians; that's just what they did. In the end, Satan is always defeated. Jesus is King and He is always victorious. Hallelujah! we get to share the victory with Jesus.

> *(To) the victor: I will give him the right to sit with*
> *Me on My throne, just as I also won the victory and*
> *sat down with My Father on His throne.*
> Revelation 3:21 (HCSB)

The truth is that Haiti is dangerous. There are lots of bugs and lots of wicked people. However, giving in to the fear of danger can't be an option. We don't have a valid reason to ever shrink back in fear "for God gave us a spirit not of fear but of power and love and self-control." (2 Timothy 1:7) We're not called to be cowards. We're called to be mighty men! We've got the ultimate weapon on our side: the Spirit of the Living God. If God is for us, what can man (or bacteria or bugs) do to us? *Nothing.*

"But I will warn you whom to fear: fear Him who, after He has killed, has authority to cast into hell. Yes, I tell you, fear Him!" (Luke 12:5) King David exhibited this as he faced Goliath. Jesus faced this as He was led to the cross. Stephen faced this as he was stoned to death as a martyr.

There are many persecuted Christians who face a life-and-death test of their faith every single day. While my faith is certainly stretched by living in Haiti, what I encounter doesn't compare with other missionaries and other doctors who serve in countries and cultures where their faith is considered anathema. For members of a home church in China, each time they convene they risk arrest and possible imprisonment. In other closed nations, Christians risk their lives to smuggle in Bibles and share their faith with fellow citizens.

In many societies there's no cultural validation or social acceptance for being a Christian; consequently, believers know that following Christ will be an upstream swim, and their faith is all the more precious because of it.

Following in the footsteps of Jesus Christ and living by faith takes more than good intentions. It takes *practice*. Loving God and obeying his Word is nothing if not *practical*. We've seen how the Bible clearly emphasizes the way God cares for his children; in fact, He cares for all His creation, even the birds of the air and the lilies of the field.

So Jesus, like His Father, focused His ministry in very practical, physical ways. He turned water into wine at a wedding celebration in Cana. He blessed a couple of fish and a handful of bread and turned it into an alfresco feast for over five thousand people. He healed lepers with his touch. He spat in the mud and made a healing paste for the blind. He washed the feet of his disciples. He made them breakfast on the beach.

Do you remember my family's daily question of, "What did you do today that required faith"? I've finally come to the conclusion that the proof of my faith is to sometimes forgo self-protection and even self-care. Faith requires me to forget about myself in order to express concern for others. Faith requires me to feed and clothe others instead of only myself and my family. Faith requires me to spend money on others instead of only myself. I take care of others . . . knowing that God takes care of me.

Faith looks like something. And it costs something. In fact, it's quite expensive. That's why it's called sacrificial faith. Faith means we've sacrificed something we thought we needed or wanted in order to spend ourselves on others.

Faith requires risk.

Faith means we take risks for the Kingdom of God.

To answer the call of Jesus for our lives, we must live like Him, walk in faith like Him, and take risks like Him in order to love like Him.

If we are not taking risks to advance the Kingdom, we are not exercising faith. When we risk our safety to rescue child slaves, risk our savings to build a hospital, or risk humiliation to spread the Gospel, the world will notice something different about us. They will see people answering the call to live and love like Jesus.

Faith means we love like Jesus, who doesn't just care *about* the poor but cares *for* the poor. There's a world of difference in those prepositions.

It's easy to say what we care *about*. Our lives show who we care *for*.

So let's ask ourselves the question: Whom do I care for? Myself or others? How would the world respond if it saw Christians acting out our faith in Jesus through our love for the poor, oppressed, and marginalized?

What's holding us back from caring for others? What limitations do we put in our lives that are keeping us from living beyond our own limits instead of leading a life that looks like the sacrificial life of Jesus Christ?

CHAPTER 18

THE PAINS OF CHILDBIRTH

To live beyond means caring for the
needs of those beyond our borders.

I BELIEVE THE GOSPEL IS BEST SPREAD BY FIRST TAKING CARE OF people's physical needs. Not only is this reflected in Jesus's ministry, it is, in fact, the process Jesus told His disciples to follow in their missions. "When you enter a town and are welcomed, eat what is offered to you. Heal the sick who are there and tell them, 'The kingdom of God has come near to you'" (Luke 10:8–9).

Isn't that a great sequence? Enter the town, heal the sick, and *then* tell them about the kingdom of God. This very command is the motivation behind our clinic, hospital, clean water initiative, and maternal health program. It's awfully hard for someone to listen to a sermon when they have a fever or their child is crying from hunger. We never want to miss a single opportunity to preach the Gospel, but first, we take care of their physical bodies, allowing their spiritual ears to open.

The church that meets each Sunday on our LiveBeyond base is flourishing. Each year, we've baptized about one hundred people. Many are former Voodou worshipers. Most had never been a part of any Christian congregation. Their hearts are wide open to the saving message of Jesus. Why? They are able to hear the truth. Their bellies are full. They are able to sit still because their scabies has been cured. Their children aren't crying from earaches. They have plenty of fresh water to drink. They are primed to hear about the Living Water, the Bread of Life, the Great Physician.

———

One day in 2017, I happened to be outside when I looked up and saw Marie approaching. Walking slowly down the rutted gravel path leading into our clinic, she struggled in the oppressive Haitian heat, holding an infant in one arm and the hand of a toddler in her other hand. Judging by her distended belly, there was another baby growing inside of her. She was obviously overburdened, both mentally and physically.

It's not that it was hotter than usual that day; it's always hot here. But as the baby grew in Marie's womb, he took the last of the nutrients out of his young mother's already depleted body and she felt it more than ever. With her time to deliver approaching, she likely remembered her other six children and how hard their births were as she cried out on the dirt floor of her mud hut. Marie would never forget the faces of her two little ones that she laid to rest in that same dirt the year before.

Marie has heard stories of women in the United States, in Florida, less than two hours away, who give birth in bright, clean hospitals and receive medicines that take away the pain. She's heard their babies are put into warm, clean beds instead of rags on the dirt floor. She knows that most of the mothers and babies there have both clean water and more than enough to eat.

But that place two hours away might as well be a million miles away. To Marie, it sounds like a different planet, a fantasy world from fairy tales. So she did what she had to do. She came to see us even when she didn't feel like making the five-mile hike beneath the sweltering tropical sun. After checking her vitals and her children's, we gave Marie prenatal vitamins, as much clean water as she could drink, and rice and beans to take home to her family.

When I watch the women in our maternal health program, I ask myself, "Why is it that two countries separated by a flight less than two hours long have such vastly different cultures?

Why are the people's stories in the States, even those we call poor, so much radically better than the majority of Haitians?"

Two worlds.

One of success and comfort and the other of fear and pain.

One with more resources than can be counted and the other with starvation, disease, and death.

Many have asked what I'm afraid of. I'm afraid of having to tell God why I would turn away young mothers like Marie without the care, nourishment, and medicine they need. I'm afraid to tell Him that the resources He intended to be spent on them were spent on me. I'm afraid I may prove that I care more about myself that I care about them.

So many young Haitian mothers fear the ordeal of childbirth without adequate water, food, and medicine for themselves and their little ones. So we started our maternal health program to combat these fears and more importantly, of course, to show the love of God to them and their babies.

Our LiveBeyond maternal health team teaches mothers about infant nutrition, hygiene, healthy practices for the mother, and how to know when to bring the baby to the doctor. We learn from these mothers as well. For instance, many of them refused the prenatal vitamins, and we weren't sure of the reasons. But one expectant mother finally explained that the vitamins made her hungry and since she didn't have enough food, she didn't want to take them. So budgets were revamped, plans were made, and we started sending the women home with a bag of beans and rice along with their weekly prenatal vitamins.

We never turn anyone away, but our resources are limited. By offering food, prenatal vitamins, medical care, and education, we strive to give mothers like Marie hope. At any given time we typically care for around three hundred pregnant women like Marie, doing our best to give them medical care similar to what American mothers get.

There are eight hundred more women within a five-mile radius of our clinic who are not in our program. And perhaps what upsets me most is the cost is only about $150 a month for each woman. For around the same price as a few nights of fine dining in the States, a woman can receive food, prenatal vitamins, and medical tests from trained Haitian doctors and nurses for an entire month.

Things that seem so trivial that we don't give them a second thought are a big deal for many other people around our world.

We all agree that when a mother or her baby does not survive childbirth, much is lost. Haiti has one of the highest maternal mortality rates in the world. Women here fear childbirth because they have all had a friend succumb to the rigors of birth.

Anyone's death is devastating to a community. But a woman who dies in childbirth not only leaves children without their mother and a husband without his wife, but she also leaves a resource-poor village to raise a child. Often this community, while willing to raise an orphan, simply doesn't have the capacity to feed another mouth. This often results in another child on the streets.

With thirty thousand orphans in Haiti already, women dying in childbirth ripples throughout the community and ultimately, the entire country. And I would add, throughout the entire world. This is not just a problem for those suffering in Haiti and a few other isolated areas. If technology has made the global community accessible across barriers of distance, language, and culture, then surely we can address the needs not only in our own backyards but backyards around the world.

No woman should die in childbirth because she lacks proper nutrition, clean water, and basic medical care. No child should begin life as an orphan when it takes so little to save his mother. I'm convinced we can reach all of the expectant women in our area.

But don't take my word about the success of the maternal health program—take Guerlanda's. She came to us through a mobile clinic long before we had purchased the land or built our clinic. She had delivered her daughter Melissa just a few weeks before, and she knew there was something wrong. During my examination of the infant, I discovered she had tracheomalacia. The cartilage that was supposed to hold open her trachea was weakened, so when she breathed in, her trachea collapsed, and she wasn't able to get enough air in her lungs. It often results in pneumonia when left untreated. I could tell that this baby would need surgery to insert a stent to fix the trachea, something she would not have access to without a medical visa to the United States. We immediately started Melissa on antibiotics to combat her pneumonia, and we took her with us to the guest house in which we were staying to observe her overnight. But most importantly, we prayed. For several days in a row, we treated her and prayed for the healing of her trachea. Because without healing, this innocent child would die.

Thanks to the grace of God, the tracheomalacia miraculously resolved.

After Guerlanda weaned Melissa, she came back to us during another mobile clinic saying, "I saw what you do, and I want to be a part of it." Guerlanda has basically been a part of the maternal health staff since its inception. She works with women just like her, her friends and family, teaching them how to better care for their babies so that their families have a brighter future.

I love to see the women in our maternal health program lined up each week for baby day. This is usually a Friday when all the new mothers bring their babies to our clinic for weigh-ins, checkups, and follow-up treatments. The women arrive early because there will be over a hundred mothers holding babies and bouncing toddlers. When I see this parade of joyful life, my heart swells. In the LiveBeyond maternal health program, we've been able to cut the perinatal mortality rate for the newborns by two-thirds simply by making sure the mothers get vitamins, clean water, education, medical care, and adequate nourishment. These women and children represent the perfect love of God casting out their fear. They no longer have to fear the nearness of death in childbirth. They can look to the future with expectant joy, knowing they and their babies will be healthy.

In the months and years to come, I envision more women and babies thriving and growing in the love of Christ, living a life without the fear of hunger, disease or death.

Years ago, I was humbled and convicted by these familiar words of Jesus:

"For I was hungry and you gave Me something to eat, I was thirsty and you gave Me something to drink, I was a stranger and you invited Me in, I needed clothes and you clothed Me, I was sick and you looked after Me, I was in prison and you came to visit Me."

Then the righteous will answer Him, "Lord, when did we see You hungry and feed You, or thirsty and give You something to drink? When did we see You a stranger and invite You in, or needing clothes and clothe You? When did we see You sick or in prison and go to visit You?"

The King will reply, "Truly I tell you, whatever you did for one of the least of these brothers and sisters of Mine, you did for Me." (Matthew 25:35–40)

My life was turned upside down when I came to understand this passage. For as long as I can remember I've wanted to know and love God. I've wanted to live a life "worthy of the Lord" (Colossians 1:10). I've wanted to hear the words, "Well done, my good and faithful servant" (Matthew 25:23). But for most of my life, I didn't realize that when I took care of the *poor*, the *hungry*, the *naked*, the *sick*, and the *imprisoned*, I was actually taking care of *Him*. So now, when I pick up a naked child or debride the scar tissue of a young man with an injured leg or care for the needs of an expectant mother, I look deep into their eyes and in my heart, I say, "I see You, Lord."

CHAPTER 19

FROM DARKNESS TO LIGHT

To live beyond means believing in the power of Christ to overcome the power of the devil.

SOMETIMES PEOPLE ASK ME WHAT I BELIEVE IS THE KEY TO TRANS-forming Haiti from a struggling state to a functioning, healthy country. Depending on their viewpoint, they might expect that I'd focus on good governance, fair elections, building the economic base, or simply that the world extend Haiti more aid. But I believe that Haiti can only be transformed as a nation if it is transformed spiritually, and that happens one life at a time. Perhaps the most obvious transition from darkness to light is best depicted through the story of one woman.

We first saw her as she hobbled down the dusty road. Gangly and rail thin, she walked with the gait of someone in chronic pain. Her dingy, threadbare red turban was wrapped loosely around her thinning hair and bore witness to her profession. She was a Voodou priestess. As she walked into our remote medical facility, the dull roar of our typically chaotic clinic was silenced by shocked gasps.

Like Moses parting the Red Sea, this unexpected visitor was given a wide berth by dozens of other Haitian villagers. Clearly, they were terrified. No one made eye contact with her. No one spoke. The crowd was silent and edged away from her, many shielding their children and babies. The seasoned volunteer medical personnel, though hardened by the assaults of urban trauma departments, had never witnessed such a spectacle. They all wondered, "Who is this woman who clearly inspires such fear in her community?"

Voodou, sometimes spelled voodoo or vodou, originally a West African religion, was transported by West African natives caught in the net of slavery cast by the French in the 1700s. It was quickly adopted in Haiti. It syncretized with the Catholic religion forced on the slaves by their French colonizers, hiding beneath this form of Christianity. In fact, for many years the

Roman Catholic Church did not recognize the Catholic Church in Haiti because of its syncretization with Voodou. The satanic practice infiltrated the island, ensnaring 70 percent of the population and becoming the lens through which Haitians see the world.

This dark practice involves incantations, herbal potions, animal (and sometimes human) sacrifices, fire, and blood. Blood used in Voodou ceremonies usually comes from chickens, goats, or pigs, the sacrificial animals of choice, but none is exempt; the only requirement is the presence of blood. Possessed adherents dancing to drummed rhythms cast the blood about, cursing the objects of their wrath and proclaiming allegiance to the evil one. As a sign of their committed devotion, true believers endure paths of fire, walking slowly over the hellish flames.

Haitian Voodou is the antithesis of Christianity. Blessings from the one are replaced by curses from the other, hope is replaced by despair, love by fear, and solace by pain. And now the very embodiment of Voodou had just walked into our clinic.

We learned her name was Maizie, and it quickly became apparent she was a true believer in the dark arts she practiced. She had walked through the fires of Voodou worship for twenty years, and her feet and legs bore the deeply seared scars of repeated rituals. That first day she displayed an odd mix of authority—clearly reflected by the crowd's fearful response—and trepidation at encountering individuals from our LiveBeyond team who held such opposing views to her own. She wanted medical help to alleviate her burns but asking required her to swallow some of her pride.

Later we would discover Maizie had fallen into the snare of the occult at a pliable young age. Convinced that Voodou worship was the true way, she quickly rose to prominence in her religion. She repeatedly broadcast her devotion to the evil one by walking through the flames, and as a result, she suffered severe fourth-degree burns. It is interesting to note that male Voodou worshippers rarely walk through fire—they have the women do it as another means of exercising control. These untreated burns had turned her feet into thick blocks and her legs into a horrific menagerie of exposed bone and tendon.

My wife, Laurie, was the first to act. As the organizer of the medical professionals in our wound-care clinic, she knew what had to be done. Though wary at first, Maizie warmed to the treatment of antibiotic creams and even to the gentle debridement, but Laurie's attempt to share the healing words of the Gospel was another matter altogether. Maizie physically recoiled from Laurie's soothing, loving message and shunned any attempts at prayer. She wanted the Americans' medication but not their religion.

So without backing down from our usual practice, Laurie saw that Maizie's wounds were treated and showed as much kindness and compassion as possible—which I think must have really confused her. Months later she told us that at the initial visit she knew something was out of the ordinary with us but also with her treatment. She'd walked the same mountain road to her hut three hours away hundreds of times before, but her journey home that day made it clear something was different.

Her legs still ached from the debridement and the soothing creams helped a lot, but her step seemed lighter. She knew that she'd been prayed for. She found the prayers unnerving, and yet she knew that something had made a difference. Whatever it was, she knew she wanted to go back to that clinic.

Each month, she found herself hiking the three hours back to our clinics eventually held at the LiveBeyond base, and each month her step became a little lighter and her burns felt a little better. Other patients still gave her a wide berth, but as they whispered among themselves, it was clear they weren't so shocked to see her there anymore. She was more receptive to our attempts at conversation, including our expressions of faith. After half a year or more of treatment, it was clear our prayers had not only become more tolerable, but Maizie indicated she actually looked forward to them.

Then one day, something truly amazing happened.

Maizie approached our clinic, almost a year to the day since her first visit. Her expression was almost pleasant, not the scowl she had worn as her mask of defense for so many years. As Laurie unwrapped her bandages and began gently removing layers of old, dead skin from her wounds, Maizie began to ask questions. They continued to talk and Maizie was clearly experiencing a shift in her thinking. The healing ointment softening her scarred legs was apparently softening her heart as well.

That day Maizie promised Laurie she would no longer worship the devil. She said she wanted to know this Jesus whose love clearly defied the kind of logic she had grown up experiencing. This former Voodou priestess now believed in Jesus and accepted Him as her Lord and Savior.

That day her long walk home seemed like only minutes. She told us later that she knew why her step felt so light. She had let go of the fears and worries that Satan used to trap her for most of her adult life. As the gentle soothing of the burn cream had healed her legs, so, too, the gentle soothing of the Lord Jesus had healed her scarred heart. She had experienced love.

Maizie is now one of our dearest friends. She's delivered a baby through our maternal health program, she comes to the LiveBeyond church on Sundays, and she comes to our clinic for continued treatment for her legs. She became a baptized believer in July 2017. Shortly after her baptism, we hired her to work in our flower gardens. Our mission team members love to climb the harrowing hill to her hut, wanting to see firsthand this woman who has been transferred from darkness to light.

Her transition was not easy. As a Voodou priestess, she was ostracized by Haitian Christians who wanted nothing to do with her or her religion. When she gave up Voodou, she gave up the rest of her community. After her baptism, the Christians in her village slowly started to warm to her, but the truth of her past will continue to affect her for the rest of her life. Yet she is always thankful for the companionship of Jesus. She is a hero and a true champion of the Christian faith. She has a better understanding of what it means to leave the power of Satan to become a follower of Jesus than I ever will.

To live beyond means to believe in the power of Christ to overcome the power of the devil. So as we fall asleep to the sound of Voodou drums beating and the shrieks of sacrificed animals, alone in the blackness of the Haitian night, I have learned to hear the Savior say, "Don't be afraid, I am here."

CHAPTER 20

EVEN UNTO DEATH

To live beyond means to remain persistent,
even in the face of overwhelming odds.

WE KNEW SHE WAS A PROSTITUTE WHEN WE HIRED HER.

When Lourde applied for a job to work with LiveBeyond taking care of the lawn, we knew that she had worked as a prostitute before. In fact, we weren't totally sure if she had given up the lifestyle at all. But we decided to hire her anyway and she was anxious to work in a new capacity.

Each day during our chapel services and at the church service on Sunday, Lourde would sit on the second row. She knew the words to every song, so we suspected that she had attended church at some point in her past. She sang with gusto in a powerful alto, loud enough so that you could pick her voice out from the crowd on occasion. When we prayed, she usually got down on her hands and knees and prayed with fervor. Her face was often stained with tears as she prayed, and when you listened closely, she was begging God for mercy. Laurie and I regularly asked her if she was ready to leave behind Voodou and become a Christian. But her answer was always the same.

"Poko." Not yet.

It made us wonder if she refused give up her nighttime job simply because she was enjoying the extra money. For several years we regularly counseled her and asked if she was ready to accept Jesus, and for years she gave us the same response.

Not yet.

Until one spring day in 2016.

It was just another day in the work week for us, but on that day, Lourde decided she was ready to leave her past behind. She told us to have everything ready for her on Sunday because she was going to accept Jesus and be baptized. We were absolutely elated for her and glad that our constant efforts had finally paid off. So we got out the baptismal robes and set aside some towels just for Lourde that Sunday. It was even more exciting because we had an American team of volunteers coming in to work in the clinic the following week, so we were happy they would get to be a part of the celebration.

On Sunday, she came in the gates very solemn but calm. When it came time for the baptism, she immediately came forward to put on her robe and prepare for the water. A common custom in Haiti, not one that we started but one that we find very encouraging, is that it is customary for a person to share their testimony before they get baptized. They confess their sins before everyone so that they can leave them behind as they become Christians. I had an idea of what Lourde was going to say, but as I translated for the group of Americans, I have to admit that her powerful testimony sent me into a bit of shock.

You see, Lourde was not just a normal prostitute.

She was a Voodou cult prostitute.

Long ago, she had signed her life to a Voodou priest *in blood* so that he could offer her services to Voodou worshipers during religious ceremonies. She had been used by people more times than she could count.

But she was ready to leave that all behind. The reason she had not come forward for so many years was because she was afraid of what the priest (houngan) would do to her when she left. When she told him that week that she was leaving Voodou forever, he promised to kill her. How dare she take away his main revenue stream!

But she said that she had come to the conclusion that she would rather live in the freedom of Jesus than in slavery of Voodou.

I was shocked at the revelation and I might not have done the best job translating everything she said to the American volunteers. I hope they got the gist. She asked me to baptize her, a request that I happily accepted.

When I brought her up out of the water, she let out a scream and went face first back down into the baptistry. I had to physically grab her and pull her back up out of the water. But when she came up the second time, her face was transformed by a sense of peace. She was ready for whatever might come her way. Her Haitian brothers and sisters went wild with rejoicing. They knew that she had just been delivered from the power of the enemy.

After church, she hugged everyone goodbye for what might be the last time. She knew she was facing her death, but she was prepared to surrender to whatever befell her. She fully expected that the Voodou priest who had owned her would kill her as soon as she got back home.

Faithful even unto death.

I have to admit, I was nervous every time my phone rang for the rest of the day. I wasn't sure if I would see her on Monday at work.

Thank the Lord that her Voodou master didn't harm her. And to this day, she continues to be a beacon of light, not only among our employees but among all of Thomazeau. Now she manages the housekeeping of the LiveBeyond school. And she sits on the second row and sings her heart out, but instead of always begging for mercy from God, she is able to have a loving relationship with Him. When I see her, I know exactly what God's love looks like. It looks like bringing this woman out of total darkness into the Kingdom of life. Even cult prostitutes can be redeemed by the blood of the Lamb. And I think she has a deeper understanding of His unfathomable love than I will ever have.

If that's not a powerful testimony I don't know what is.

I am so honored to be part of her story. But I'm more inspired than anything. I'm inspired by her courage to face the very real threat of death. I'm impressed by her tenacity and persistence to follow the Lord through even the most over-whelming odds. And I'm in awe of the transformation that God has worked in her and through her. She is one of the best mothers I know, a pillar in her community, and she is truly my friend. When I read Galatians 2:20, I hear her voice: "I have been crucified with Christ. It is no longer I who live, but Christ who lives in me. And the life I now live in the flesh I live by faith in the Son of God, who loved me and gave Himself for me." Lourde shares the love of Jesus with everyone she meets, and because of her testimony, people know they can trust her when she tells them about who God is. Just as God is using me for His purpose, He redeemed her and is using her too. He is ready to use all of us for His good. The question is,

Are you ready?

CHAPTER 21

THE EMBODIMENT
OF GOD

*To live beyond means operating in the power of the
Spirit in order to be God's hands and feet in this world.*

"FATHER OF THE FATHERLESS AND THE PROTECTOR OF WIDOWS IS God in His holy habitation" (Psalm 68:5).

At first glance, this is a passage that we would read and simply nod in agreement. "Yes," we would say, "God is the Father of the fatherless and protector of widows. That's who our God in Heaven is." But let's look deeper. *Where* is God's holy habitation? Heaven is a correct answer. But for Spirit-filled believers, God's holy habitation is in *us*!

We are the holy habitation of God.

That means that for God to be the Father of the fatherless and the protector of widows, *we* must be the father of orphans and caretaker of widows. By God's mysterious design, through the empowerment of His Holy Spirit, we represent God for who He is, and without us, His work just doesn't get done.

We often pray, "God, protect the orphans. Give food to the hungry. Help the poor and needy." And He's saying, "That's your job! It won't get done unless you do it!"

We seem to think that if we pray, there will be a mystical blessing that floats down over the orphans and brings them protection. That blessing may come, but guess what? That blessing has a name. It's you. It's me. It's anyone with the Spirit of God who chooses to be like Him, to act like Him, to love like Him, and to live like Him. Without His people choosing to be His representatives on earth, His work will not get done.

I can just hear the arguments. People will say, "God is great. God can do anything He wants, with or without us." And those statements are absolutely right. But for some amazingly holy reason, God has chosen to put His Spirit inside His people *in order* to get His work done. Does He have to use you? No. Does He have to use me? No. But He chooses to use *someone*. That's His plan. That's His design.

In fact, He searches for people like you and me to help Him accomplish His work. "For the eyes of the Lord run to and fro throughout the whole earth, to give strong support to those whose heart is blameless toward Him." (2 Chronicles 16:9) And through us, He can accomplish even greater works than those He gave to Jesus. In John 14:12 Jesus says, "Truly, truly, I say to you, whoever believes in Me will also do the works that I do; and greater works than these will he do, because I am going to the Father."

Can you believe that? Believers can do, not only the works of Jesus but even *greater* works than the ones He did. I still have a hard time wrapping my head around that one.

———

I realize that while all of us were created equal, we were not all given equal circumstances. The parable of the talents in Matthew 25 is evidence of this. One servant was given five talents, another two, and the third servant was given one talent. I know that I was one of the lucky ones with five talents. I have been blessed with a loving Christian home, a top-notch education, an exciting career, and a supportive family. Therefore, I see it as a personal responsibility as a servant to the King to use my talents to the best of my abilities. That's why I'm in Haiti. And to be honest, after seeing the poverty and oppression that is so prevalent in Haiti, it seems like most of us who were born into developed countries were all given more than one talent. There is a safety net of welfare and medical care services available in the United States that makes much of the world envious. No, that doesn't make up for people with a terrible family life or little access to education or any other number of problems, but it is something.

But whether we have five talents or two talents or even one, we should seize the opportunity to make the most of what we were given. I know that I don't want to miss out on hearing this response from the Master at the end of the road: "Well done, good and faithful servant. You have been faithful over a little; I will set you over much. Enter into the joy of your Master." (Matthew 25:21, 23) The joy of the Master is a gift from God that I will not only feel in Heaven but in my heart now while I serve as well. I encourage you, fellow Christians, to do good works, be that in Haiti or the United States or the rest of the world. Then you, too, will receive the overwhelming joy of the Master!

———

There is no hope for Haiti, or any other country, except in Jesus Christ. So we love to ask, "How do you get Jesus Christ to Haiti? Can you put Him in a container and ship Him there?"

Amazingly, the answer is yes!

You are the container of the Lord Jesus Christ!

You are the embodiment of God who gives the orphan a home, the widow a caretaker, the pregnant woman medical attention. You are the one who binds up the wounds of the injured, who rubs salve on the infected, who extracts teeth from the miserable. You are the one who teaches a child to pray and sing. You are the one who takes food to a starving family. You are the one who sings with the blind, holding the hand of the ill as they die. You are the one who comforts a father at the funeral of his daughter. You are the one who provides jobs and a future for young men. You are the one teaching leadership skills to boys and girls. You are the one bringing shoes so that children can go to school.

You are the embodiment of the Father—the protector, the provider, the encourager, the teacher, the great physician, the counselor, the comforter.

When we do His work, we glorify God. "In the same way, let your light shine before others, so that they may see your good works and give glory to your Father who is in Heaven." (Matthew 5:16) So how does our light shine into the world? Through our good works. Why do we do these works? To give glory to the Father. God receives glory because we do His works. He has put His Spirit inside a body: my body, your body, and together we are the body of Christ. And the body of Christ does the works of God.

What a high calling!

I love to watch people filled with the Spirit of God bring relief to the poor in Haiti. Each year, close to six hundred Christians come to spend a week or more on the LiveBeyond base, bringing with them kindness, compassion, medications, education, innovations, and love. Laurie and I literally feel the spiritual water table rise with the flood of these godly men and women.

Many times, Laurie and I have personally experienced the kindness of God that comes through His children. Suspecting our need for encouragement, people come with just the right word, a thoughtful gift, or best of all, the time to listen. Through this, we receive the boost and support we so badly need. I can't tell you how much it means to us when our friends from high school and college take time out of their busy schedules to come work alongside us in Haiti. I love getting to work alongside qualified doctors and nurses and other medical professionals in Haiti during clinic hours. And Laurie loves it when teachers volunteer a week out of their busy schedules to come work with our Kè Pou Timoun children. That still says nothing about the tireless efforts of the physical and occupational therapists who have come on mission trips to develop individualized plans for each of our Johnny's Kids.

I can't even begin to describe the stress relief for me personally when qualified plumbers and electricians come to Haiti to use their talents to help us keep the base running. When we first moved to Haiti, I was getting out of bed every night to deal with the pesky generator. Thanks to our team of volunteer electricians, I am getting a lot more sleep! These volunteers are using their gifts and talents to relieve oppression in Haiti.

And with new technology available to us, people in the United States can now share their talents with the people of Haiti without ever having to leave home. Each week, we have American preachers, teachers, businessmen, and farmers teaching classes via Skype to Haitians. The preachers discuss the Bible and help Haitian pastors from across Haiti find solutions for church problems. Teachers offer English as a Second Language classes to children in the Kè Pou Timoun program. Businessmen offer a financial responsibility class to teach Haitians how to save money and pay off debts. And my son David teaches appropriate technology and agriculture classes to local farmers via Skype and in-person seminars. It has been a great way for past team members to continue working with their friends in Haiti even when they can't devote the resources to spend a week in Haiti with us. And it offers those who are not able to Haiti a way to serve and connect with the Haitian people.

The Haitians who attend the classes are thankful for the love and support they receive from their American friends. They know that education is something that can't be taken away from them, regardless of the poverty they face every day. Both Americans and Haitians are blessed by this avenue of interaction. And these educational opportunities get us one step closer to making a tangible, sustainable difference in the community of Thomazeau.

———

God uses each of us to accomplish different goals, according to His will. God uses me and several members of the LiveBeyond team to bring medical care, clean water, and maternal health to Thomazeau, Haiti, so that Thomazeau will be transformed for the Kingdom of God. He uses Laurie and a team of Haitians and Americans to bring about care for the disabled through our At Risk, Kè Pou Timoun, and Johnny's Kids programs. He uses Jacklyn and our Haitian preacher known widely as Pastor Sargesse to evangelize to and disciple men and women in Thomazeau. He uses David to teach agriculture classes and John Mark to teach about financial responsibility. And He uses thousands of volunteers each year to supplement our ongoing mission work in Haiti through short-term trips.

I enjoy listing these ways that my loved ones serve but I know also that God is calling each of you to be His hands and feet in your community and abroad. How can you best respond to this call?

CHAPTER 22

THE KING'S RETURN

To live beyond means to actively prepare
for the Return of the King.

A few years ago, Laurie and I made the decision to read the book of Revelation every Saturday in celebration of the Sabbath. We aren't sure how long we will do this, but we have enjoyed this time together in the Bible each week. We sit together on our porch overlooking the LiveBeyond demonstration farm or in our living room, alternating between readers. Sometimes we have other people join us. Our international interns have joined us during the summer months. We've read it so many times that Laurie and I have memorized many of the chapters. And yet we still find ourselves asking questions, wondering about certain passages, and seeking answers from the Lord.

We do this because Laurie and I fully expect the Lord to come back during our lifetime, and we are preparing for His triumphal return. A common theme we've noticed throughout our readings is the "fine white linen." The faithful believers in Sardis are clothed with white garments (3:4–5). The twenty-four elders around the throne wear white garments and crowns (4:4). The martyrs slain for the word of God are given white robes as they rest beneath the altar (6:9). The great multitude from every nation stands before the throne and the Lamb in white robes (7:9). The Heavenly armies are clothed in fine, white linen as they follow the Rider of the White Horse into battle (19:14). And, most importantly, the Bride of Christ—the Church—is clothed "with fine linen, bright and pure for the fine linen is the righteous deeds of the saints." (19:8)

When the King returns, He will be ready for His Bride, the Church. And she will be ready for Him, dressed in fine linen—her bridal clothes. But the amazing part is that the linen she wears, that all of us wear, is made up of *the righteous deeds of the saints*. Her bridal clothes are our deeds.

So do our deeds matter to the Kingdom?

Absolutely!

Our deeds aren't what save us, God's grace does that, but they do make an actual difference in the Kingdom. And God invites us into His work. How cool is that?

This passage gives me hope in the future of the Kingdom of God. Jesus is my example of how to work to achieve that future. Laurie and I want to hasten the day of the return of the King. We want to help get everyone—especially the people of Thomazeau, but really all around the world—ready for His return. And frankly, we aren't ready yet. There is still more work to be done. So all of us at LiveBeyond are doing everything we can to hasten the Day!

In 2 Corinthians 9:6–8, it says: "The point is this: whoever sows sparingly will also reap sparingly, and whoever sows bountifully will also reap bountifully. Each one must give as he has decided in his heart, not reluctantly or under compulsion, for God loves a cheerful giver. And God is able to make all grace abound to you, so that having all sufficiency in all things at all times, you may abound in every good work."

God does not sow sparingly into us. He sows bountifully and He reaps bountifully in His harvest. God enables us as the Church to sow and reap bountifully because He made *all* grace abound to us, so that we, being sufficient in all things at all times, can abound in every good work. God gives the Church everything she needs through His grace so that she is free to cheerfully give.

If we answer the call to serve as a conduit of God's blessings, including our money and material possessions, then our lifestyle and priorities—both large and small—will reflect a mindset of giving, not possessing. This means that we approach God's abundance with open hands, giving freely and generously to those in need. This kind of investment in the Kingdom reaps eternal rewards, expanding God's presence in the lives of others, and keeping our hearts focused on our greatest love.

This passage reinforces our role as distributors of wealth, not hoarders. This Scripture doesn't say, "God is able to make *some* grace abound to you so that having *some* sufficiency in *some* things at *some* times you may abound in *some* good works." No! He says *all* grace abounds to us so that having *all* sufficiency in *all* things at *all* times we may abound in *every good work* (v. 8).

Sometimes we read the one but think the other. We read of His full grace and sufficiency, there for us at all times enabling us to participate in every good work, but we don't believe Him. We assume He really just means that *sometimes* He'll give us a little more than we actually need so that we can share our leftovers. But God gives us *all* we need so that we can then provide for others. This includes His grace, mercy, and compassion. We experience God's blessings, mercy, and grace in order to pass these gifts on to others.

Once again, I see God talking specifically about works. God provides His grace to us (supply) and we pour it out on others in need (demand). This passage goes on to make it clear that this same principle applies to material wealth as well (2 Corinthians 9:10–11). God enlarges our harvest in order to increase our capacity for generosity. He gives me the ability to make money (Deuteronomy 8:18) so that I will be fully sufficient and can produce good works. He supports me emotionally, physically, and spiritually so that I am sufficient and can produce good works for His glory. In other words, we're made rich so we can give it away!

I was named after my father, but I still enjoy reading about our original namesake from the Bible, King David. He was a man after God's own heart, a fierce warrior, a musician, and a shepherd. As king of Israel, it was David's desire to build a place for the Lord, a temple as His dwelling place. He did not feel right about living in a house of cedar while the ark of God was in a tent (2 Samuel 7:1–2). While God later denied David the permission to build the temple because of the blood on his hands, David still did everything in his power to prepare for his son Solomon to build it. He made the plans for the temple's construction; he gathered the materials; he purchased the Temple Mount; he instructed his son Solomon regarding the task at hand. He even wrote these words: "I will not give sleep to my eyes or slumber to my eyelids, until I find a place for the Lord, a dwelling place for the Mighty One of Jacob." (Psalm 132:4–5) I like to think of this as David's mission statement. He refused to "sleep" until he accomplished everything that the Lord had prepared for him to do during his lifetime. And the amazing thing is that he reached his goal: "For David, after he had served the purpose of God in his own generation, fell asleep and was laid with his fathers." (Acts 13:36)

Jesus had a mission statement too. At the beginning of His ministry on earth after He was tempted in the desert by Satan, He entered the synagogue and read these words from the scroll of Isaiah:

"The Spirit of the Lord is upon Me,
because He has anointed Me
to proclaim good news to the poor.
He has sent Me to proclaim liberty to the captives
and recovering of sight to the blind,
to set at liberty those who are oppressed,
to proclaim the year of the Lord's favor." (Luke 4:18–19)

And that's exactly what He did. Jesus proclaimed the good news to the poor when He preached to the masses. He set free the captives in a variety of contexts. He restored the sight of the blind, both literally and figuratively. He relieved those who were oppressed by demons and society. And He constantly proclaimed the year of the Lord, the coming of the Kingdom of Heaven. Jesus came to give life and give it abundantly (John 10:10). He accomplished this by doing the work He said He would do in His mission statement in Luke 4.

To be like Jesus, I want to help others find the abundant life they will only find through Jesus. I knew that when I moved to Haiti that my purpose, my mission statement, was to transform Thomazeau for the Kingdom of God. That is how God had me working for His return. That mission is what has kept me going when dangers lurk, sleep is fleeting, and the pressures of being a missionary creep up, especially when the generator goes out at 2 a.m. It is worth all of that to serve my purpose in my generation. The joy I get when I see healthy mothers and babies coming to church on Sunday at the base is unparalleled. I'm not only part of God's work to relieve oppression, but the people we affect through LiveBeyond are giving God the glory He so richly deserves. I am fulfilling the work the Lord gave to me—work to prepare for the coming Kingdom.

Many of us haven't really thought about our walk with Jesus as a mission. We have tended to see it as a walk with God, meandering through life on a journey with no real direction. But if King David, and, more importantly, Jesus both had a mission statement, then why shouldn't we?

What is your mission statement?

I ask this question a lot in our morning Bible studies at the base when we have teams of volunteers. We want them to have something to take home at the end of the week that really matters. I like to really stretch people. I ask them to look beyond their responsibility to their families because even the most dedicated atheists do that. Reaching out to our family is an important step, don't get me wrong, but so many times people limit themselves to these goals when they have the potential to reach even further. Jesus called us to go into *all* the world, so I ask our volunteers to look inside themselves to discover how they can live beyond their own lives for the outsider, the captive, the oppressed.

Some of our volunteers already have mission statements. Others find their purpose through some serious soul searching in Haiti and back at home. I've even had people join in my purpose to transform Thomazeau by committing to coming back to Haiti a certain number of times each year on mission trips. One church leader has committed to serve his purpose by continuing to bring teams to work with us.

So now I ask you: What is *your* mission statement, your purpose in God's Kingdom? What can *you* do to prepare the Bride for the return of the King?

So I'm going to end this book like I end each of LiveBeyond staff meetings. "Now let's get out there and LiveBeyond!"

"Every so often, it all comes together. The faith, the skill, the heart, the opportunity—it all cooperates to create a person and a story so divine that only God could make it happen. This is one of those stories. David Vanderpool is one of those people. We are blessed to have him inspire us."

—Max Lucado
Pastor and Author

"Dr. Vanderpool is changing thousands of lives, including mine. I'm honored to work with him, leave my comfort zone, and learn what it truly means to live beyond."

—Brad Paisley
Critically Acclaimed Singer,
Songwriter, Guitarist, and Entertainer

"The work and ministry of David Vanderpool, his family, and the teams who labor alongside them have changed the lives of countless thousands of people. They are living examples of what it means to 'live beyond.'"

—The Honorable William H. Frist, MD
Heart and Lung Transplant Surgeon
and Former US Senate Majority Leader

Laurie and Johnny

The Vanderpools

Mobile Medical Disaster Relief responds to Hurricane Katrina.

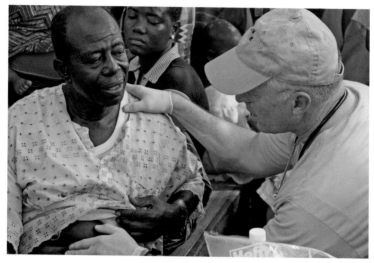

Dr. Vanderpool treats village Chief Parka in Ghana.

David hugs Kwame, one of the children rescued from slavery in Ghana.

Dr. Vanderpool treats patients in Mozambique.

Dr. Vanderpool sends medical supplies to Mozambique.

Dr. Vanderpool checks an X-ray on a home visit in Honduras.

The MMDR team visits Bobby and the children at the orphanage.

Dr. Vanderpool and the 11 boys after their hernia repair surgeries.

*John Mark and Dr. Vanderpool leave for
Haiti in response to the earthquake.*

Hell on earth

Dr. Vanderpool treats an elderly patient in the earthquake aftermath.

Post-Earthquake rubble in Port-au-Prince, Haiti.

The Palace in Haiti after the earthquake

The Vanderpool family enjoys serving together in Haiti post-earthquake.

David and John Mark relax for a few moments while working in the clinic immediately after the earthquake.

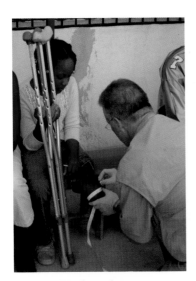

Dr. Vanderpool measures Jovanica for a prosthetic leg.

John Kely Garçon

The Bird Lady

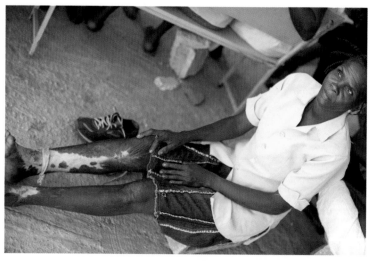

Maizie, a former Vodou priestess, rests in the clinic.

Guerlanda and Melissa

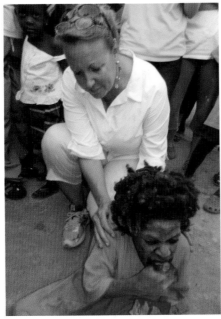

*Laurie meets Corrine
for the first time.*

Jacklyn holds a young child on a community visit.

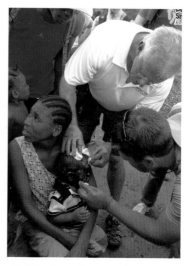

Dr. Vanderpool treats a burn victim on a community visit in Haiti.

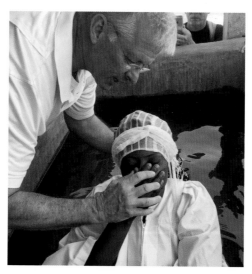

Dr. Vanderpool baptizes Lourde.

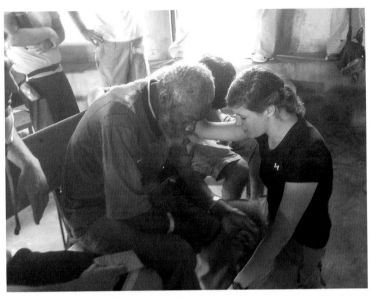

Jacklyn prays for a voodoo priest.

Laurie visits with Ramon, his grandmother, and another family member.

TiCherline

*Widler gives
John Mark and
Lauren a goat as a
wedding present.*

Connor prays for a woman after her treatment in the LiveBeyond clinic.

Children in the Kè Pou Timoun program study a children's Bible.

David and his fellow agriculture workers take a short break.

*Devin teaches a Creole literacy class
to LiveBeyond employees.*

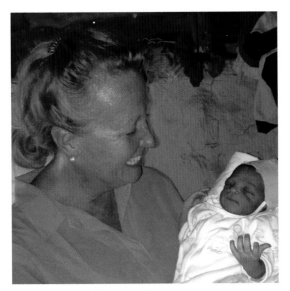

Laurie admires a newborn on a home visit.

*Dr. Vanderpool treats a patient in
the LiveBeyond clinic.*

*Gene Stallings and daughter Laurie with a member
of the Johnny's Kids program and his father.*

The working LiveBeyond base